Insightful Comments

"A great marketing guide for small business management."
Peter Bretchger- Intergrated Marketing Works

"A much needed addition to the discipline of Marketing. It takes us to the heart of the matter as to why business can't succeed with out it."   Peter Johns - Johns Design Group

"An excellent primer for any business manager or owner who must be reminded that business is all about marketing."
Jason Orr - Optimal Performance Group

Why My Company Needs Integrated Marketing Now!

A Modern Business Parable at CONE Inc.

A journey of business discovery using marketing to move your company, and its products and services to the next level of volume, revenue and profit.

R. Stephen Rayfield

First Edition

ESIL Publishing, North York, Ontario, Canada

Why My Company Needs Integrated Marketing Now!
A Modern Business Parable at CONE Inc.

By R. Stephen Rayfield

Published by:
ESIL Publishing,
213 Franklin Avenue
North York ON M2N 1C8 Canada

Rayfield, R. Stephen
Why My Company Needs Integrated Marketing Now!
A Modern Business Parable at CONE Inc. / Stephen Rayfield

ISBN 0-9683356-0-8
1. Marketing - Management. 2. Business - Marketing.
3. Small business - Management. I Title
Includes bibliographical references and index

Acknowledgments

My sincere thanks to:

Connie Baher for bringing a sense of reality to the review and solid constructive thoughts.

Peter Bretchger who traveled with the draft across many times zones and then provided timeless input.

Al Coke who unlocked the juggernaut of how to set out this message and then provided sound advice on the story.

Graham Denton for his reassuring comments and skillful handling of improvements.

Dennis Glavin for his insights and assistance in evolving the story to a higher level.

Carol Groves for looking at the story, giving me honest comments and encouraging me to publish.

Margaret Hooper for her skill in editing the thoughts on paper from concept to book.

Paul Myles who having been there, provided assurance the story was worth while publishing.

Jason Orr for his support in my career, input to this first published book and motivation to just do it.

Peter Sulmon who first and foremost gave sound advice on the concept of this book.

Peter Johns who has inspired me to seek the Why of marketing and added his enormous artistic talent to the cover design and copy editing of my first book.

Very Special Thanks

Gerry Henderson who coached, inspired, demanded and befriended me along the route of this book.

To all those people who have participated in my AMA/CMC seminars across North America. Their input, thoughts and support added to the need that inspired me to help them with this book. In addition, they have assisted me in refining my thoughts and concepts helping to turn them into useful terms and models for all business people.

Also, to the many clients who have worked so hard to use marketing to improve their business equity. Their support of my models in the real world environment is greatly appreciated. May they continue to have great career and business success.

Elizabeth Rayfield who gave the right level of faith to this project and then typed the original manuscript and final proof.

About the Author R. Stephen Rayfield

R. Stephen Rayfield is a
Marketing Coach and
President of ESIL, an
interim marketing
consulting firm, which
creates and manages
business marketing
programs and marketing
system processes.

Living in Toronto, he has traveled in North America
on business assignments, speaking, and mentoring.

His unique business background includes working for
Fortune 100 companies such as General Mills; Ralston
Purina; and Hiram Walker plus Canada Post Corporation,
and Teleglobe Insurance Systems. He has gained extensive
hands-on experience in such business areas as Marketing
Coaching, Strategic Planning Cycles, Competitive Planning,
and New Product or Service Systems Development.

He is a Keynote Speaker in both National and International
forums. Steve is a course leader for the American
Management Association on several four day seminars
including "How to be a Successful Product Manager",
"Fundamentals of Marketing", and a speaker in other
Marketing Programs.

His latest major project is writing this book after many
people throughout North America asked him *"help me tell
my boss why we need marketing."*

FORWARD

There are many books that describe how to market your company. This is not one of those books. Instead this work proves a case for why marketing is a critical element for managing a successful business. It helps you understand the real value of marketing for your company, regardless if you are big or small, new or established, private or public.

Many people think they are correctly marketing their capabilities and abilities, but they are not. They do not really understand this thing called 'Marketing' and what value it holds for all shareholders.

This book describes a mythical company called CONE Inc. and its need to grow. The president becomes aware that the missing link to his business formula is the absence of a strong integrated marketing plan. Armed with this new information, he sets out on a journey to fill in the critical information.

The president is joined on his journey of discovery by another senior staff member. They explore and are guided through the marketing process by a third person with the wisdom of business and actual marketing experience. Together they make delightful journey, chapter by chapter, to explore the key elements of the critical area of marketing.

Enjoy your read of this interesting business parable. It provides you with understandings of the key role marketing plays in the complex, but fundamental business techniques. The sound learning and specific formulas in each chapter, will assist you to make integrated marketing work for you and your business.

Dr. Alfred M. Coke, Ph.D.

Senior Partner

Dean, Dzierzawiec & Coke, Inc.

1

As he walked passed his office door he glanced at the name plate, Adam Jeffrey, President CONE Inc.

I really have a key business stumbling block he thought. Sitting in the chair behind the cluttered desk he stretched for the phone. Before he reached the number pad the door opened and Sarah Pounder, the CONE CFO, walked into his office.

"Adam did you get a chance this weekend to think about the third quarter figures and the year end projections I gave you late Friday?" asked Sarah.

"Yes, and it confirmed our conversation of early last week. We have a major issue and I just do not know how to address it."

"Well, "said Sarah in her usual matter of fact way "let's talk and see if we can put some shape around the business issue."

"We are just not growing fast enough and I don't know why. That's the real issue!" declared Adam.

"So what are the plusses and minuses?" she returned.

Adam took a breath and said "Let's get you a coffee, me some tea and do some more talking. This is important and I feel strongly that we need to get to the bottom of it. I need to get a handle on this issue to lead the company to the next level of development in terms of volume and profits."

On the way to get the coffee and tea, Sarah mentally reviewed what had sparked this issue. The third quarter sales figures had shown they were still growing but only by 2%, barely matching the industry. John Evergreen, one of the more vocal members of the board of directors, had mentioned recently over lunch they were hoping that CONE Inc. would really get up and grow to the next level economically. Management had the Boards support if they could just move toward solid double digit sales growth, after being flat for several years.

They also needed to generate a specific ROI the Board had set.

As Sarah sat down at the round table in his office they both looked out the window at the large pine trees behind the CONE Inc. headquarters. As they gathered their thoughts they both knew this was a key meeting. They just had to get a handle on this business issue.

Adam got up, moved to the flip chart and began. "If we look around we can say:

1. We have moved from one product to many products.

2. We have a solid management team in place, who work well together.

3. Sales are working hard and we have seen they really try.

4. Our products are a mix of different share levels in their various markets and are really all great quality.

5. The people in the company seem motivated.

6. Our client list is growing.

7. And our distribution is solid"

"So we seem to have all the business structure and elements to grow but it is just not happening," noted Sarah looking at the seven items Adam had written on the flipchart.

"We also have done a good job of reviewing where we are in terms of the competitive products in the market," mentioned Adam as he too looked at the seven points.

Both of them went quiet as they looked at the list and just could not see how to move to the next level. At last Adam had an idea and broke the silence with a thought.

"We need someone who can help us see the picture a different way, Sarah."

"You know Adam, that neighbour of mine that moved in this past July is a guy with lots of business experience and he is going to teach business at the university this fall."

"He said if I ever need any help he would be glad to give it. My husband and I helped his family when they moved in and have helped them find their way around the city. Why don't I talk to him tonight and see if we can set something up to get some insight on this issue?"

"Tell me more about him," asked Adam with some interest.

"Well he has a business background in several different industries. He recently decided to change careers rather than retire. He has always been interested in learning and felt he could help students get started with real world experience plus *some book stuff*, as he calls it. He feels strongly about giving back some of the ideas, concepts and practical things he has learned in his career.

But he really talks about the results needed, not just theory or academic models of business. Adam I really feel an hour with him would be worth it."

He trusted Sarah's business judgment. For a finance person she had a good sense of key business options and reality, not just numbers, and an hour to perhaps get some insight was worth the investment.

Adam realized they had not been able to find the answers with their experience so maybe someone else with a different perspective could give them some new thoughts.

The next day Adam read the e-mail from Sarah. Her neighbour Peter McPhadden would be glad to meet with them. He had suggested that since the college was midway between their home and the office, he could meet at say 10:30 am on Wednesday in his office at the university.

Adam quickly checked his schedule on his computer and noted there was a meeting for that time, however he was really starting to feel instinctively that the issue was growing important and he rescheduled it, then he confirmed the Peter McPhadden meeting with Sarah.

What do I want out of the meeting he thought? Well, he would just meet him, get some of his background and see if he could really help.

2

As Adam and Sarah entered Peter's office they observed it to be a fairly business-like atmosphere, unlike what they expected from a university professor. Peter rose to meet them. He was dressed as any business president would be in a Fortune 500 company with a blue suit and red striped tie.

"Welcome to my office".

Adam thought to himself, 'He is fairly formal, I hope this is going to work.'

"Please" said Peter "have a seat and let's get comfortable. I have coffee or tea, and let's just see if I can help you."

Adam started the conversation by saying, "We have an issue we need some help on, but first I would like to understand a little bit about your background."

Peter said, "Sure, I started in sales out of university and after a couple of years was running a small sales group in one of the divisions of my company. We sold industrial products and I was enjoying it. However, an opportunity came up to move into Marketing and I had always felt I wanted to get into that area, so I tried it out. That is when I really found that I enjoyed business. I could wrap my arms around all the components that make products happen."

"After a couple of years, I moved over to a package goods company that produced candies. The division I was in manufactured boxed chocolates, like the kind you get at Christmas, Easter or Mother's Day, and some regular candies. It helped me to really focus on a different way of Marketing and to understand fully, the solid basics. We had all the same business techniques as my previous job, like advertising, trade shows, pricing, only they were focused on consumers.

From there I moved to VP Marketing at a different kind of company that worked in the not-for-profit area. We developed programs and secured merchandise for schools and helped them to sell the items to make money."

"You know when those school kids come around selling light bulbs, garden tools or chocolate bars, things like that. It was an interesting company and I helped to grow it by tripling the sales revenues in the seven years I worked there."

"I reached that golden time when retirement was coming on and decided to move to this town. My wife and I have always liked this area. There was the opportunity to move into teaching at the university. I have a lot of business background and I think if I can combine that with some book stuff it will give the students a really good start. I know when I went to college, my mentor was a business man who taught part-time and ran his own business and he always gave me different insights, rather than just the straight academic models."

He paused and then said, "So that is my business background, now please tell me a little bit about you and your company Adam."

For the next fifteen minutes, Adam and Sarah provided some solid details about CONE Inc. They covered in some detail the seven key items they had noted on the flip chart during the meeting in Adam's office. After noting each item, they talked about what they had uncovered in their analysis.

CONE Inc. was an interesting company, having grown from two smaller companies into one larger company. Peter quickly understood it had grown to a point where they needed some business help if they were to grow to the next level of sales revenue and profit.

"Well Adam, I think one of the big issues is you have grown to the point where you need that all important business discipline called Marketing."

Adam stated, "Well, we all do Marketing now, we talk to the customers and we have trade show stuff, we do brochures and sometimes we do advertising. Last year we did a PR program for a new item we launched"

"I know, but what you really need to do is think of Marketing as a set of business methodologies. There are many tools in the Marketing area that can be used to help business grow. But first we have to decide what Marketing is," stated Peter in a matter of fact way.

"Let me give you some things to think about in this area and then maybe we could meet tomorrow, or the next day and flesh it out. How would that be Adam?"

"Well I am not really sure, just yet about this Marketing thing. I don't understand why it is so important," said Adam.

"Okay," said Peter "let us start easy. We have identified all the things that are working in the company or we think are working in the company, right?"

"Right," said Adam.

"We have done a pretty solid review of CONE Inc. ," added Sarah "We know we are doing a lot of good things. But some how they do not seem to be working as strong as we expected."

"That's right," said Peter "Now you need to bring what Marketing does as a business tool, and that is focus. Marketing is a number of things. It allows you to focus products. It allows you to understand customer needs. And it allows you to understand when to get rid of products."

"But aren't we all doing Marketing now?" Adam said, looking quickly at Sarah.

Sarah replied, "I think so, but I am not really sure, we have never really defined what Marketing is at CONE Inc."

Peter then suggested, "Let's start by doing a short survey that I used to use at the Candy Company. Whenever we bought a new company, we used it to find out what they thought Marketing was, the survey was created by an outside Marketing company. We found it a very effective tool to understand what level of Marketing the new company was really at, and what the next development steps should be, for the new group. You need to be careful that we don't try to do things that are too sophisticated or too academic, when what is really needed is the simple thing."

"The simple thing?" asked Sarah inquisitively.

"We have to remember Henry Ford. 'You can buy any car you want as long as it is a Model T, and any color you want as long as it is black'. That was simple, straight forward, and focused. So let's not go off and get into multiple colors and multiple ways, when all we need is the Model T." Peter injected. " Or equally important, we do not want to use complex models when we need the fundamental techniques."

"I am going to give you this survey to fill out, and when you are ready to talk about it, call and we will set a time."

Adam seemed to hesitate, then said, "Okay, we will do the survey. Why don't we set a time next Monday."

Peter got up and printed off two copies of the survey from his computer and handed one copy to Adam and one to Sarah.

"It is important you each do the survey separately to give it a broader perspective of what is being done at CONE Inc.," stated Peter. "I have found them most effective when several people in a company do them. You will be surprised how close you both are in your individual scoring!"

Adam reviewed the six sheets of questions and commented, "This will not take long. Maybe we can meet by Friday?"

Looking at his schedule Peter answered, "1:30 - 2:00 o'clock would be fine." Adam replied he could do it, if they were to meet at his office since he had several Friday meetings scheduled. Sarah was fine with meeting at CONE Inc.

On the way back, Adam talked to Sarah, "I am not sure if this is the right thing yet. I think we need to dig into it a little deeper at the meeting." Sarah continued, "Well let's do the questions in the survey. Then decide how we feel and what we want to do."

When Adam returned to his office, he pulled out the marketing survey and thought, I'll do this tonight at home, when I can really think about it and tucked it into his take home briefcase.

3

Later that night he sat down in his den with a hot tea and devoted 30 minutes to carefully think about the answers pertaining to his company for the Marketing Effectiveness Survey ™ [1]. The questions covered a variety of areas.

The first question clearly set the tone for the survey:

1. Does management recognize the importance of designing the company to serve the needs and wants of chosen markets?

> Management primarily thinks in terms of selling current and new products to whoever will buy them. _____ 0

> Management thinks in terms of serving a wide range of markets and needs with equal effectiveness. _____ 1

> Management thinks in terms of serving the needs and wants of well-defined markets, chosen for their long-run growth and profit potential for the company. _____ 2

"Each has a rating and needs to have an answer. And I have to answer 0 or 1 or 2 as a rating for each question. OK I can do this." Adam muttered out loud.

By the time he came to question 4 he was not feeling very good about CONE Inc. This was really telling him some key information about where their company was in its lifecycle of business development and Marketing in particular.

He wondered how Sarah was doing with her survey?

He looked at question 4.

4. Is there high-level Marketing integration and control of the major Marketing functions?

> No. Sales and other Marketing functions are not integrated at the top and there is some unproductive conflict. ____ 0

> Somewhat. There is formal integration and control of the major Marketing functions, but less than satisfactory co-ordination and co-operation. _____ 1

> Yes. The major Marketing functions are effectively integrated. _____ 2

This survey was very effective in setting out some key areas. He moved quickly through the next few questions.

And then the questionnaire started to move into the area of new products. "Great," he thought, "we do this just fine. But we really don't seem to get any big home runs. Well maybe this survey will help get some."

7.How well organized is the new product development process?

> The system is ill-defined and poorly handled. _____   0

> The system exists, but lacks sophistication._____   1

> The system is well structured and professionally staffed.

_____   2

The scores were not feeling very high, but he gamely moved on answering the questions.

'Peter was right when he said this would help bring some key perspective to where CONE Inc. was currently at, and what were the key areas they needed to focus on to move to the next level of business success.' thought Adam.

The next area of the survey was that of finance and he felt confident that CONE Inc. would score high. As he read over the question and began to note the trend of the scores, he was not so sure.

11. How well does management know the sales potential and profitability of different market segments?

They did not really look at market segments. He felt a little odd. There was so much more to this area of Marketing than he had first thought.

He was starting to see how effective the survey tool was. It not only showed what they did well, but also showed what were areas for improvement.

At the end of the survey he realized their company was only scoring 7 out of 30, which meant they were poor at Marketing. Now he really needed to understand what Marketing was and what the value would be to his company.

He looked forward to the Friday meeting when he could discuss more with Peter. More importantly he was interested to see how Sarah had scored her Marketing Effectiveness Survey TM (1).

The next morning he got the answer as Sarah walked in and said, "Well I am not a numbers person all the time. I did that survey last night and, wow, I scored us 8 out of 30. We really need to look at this Marketing thing and try to understand what it is and how it can work for us."

"You're right Sarah!" Spoke Adam with spirit. "Let us review our scores and see how we rated the various questions. Then we can be prepared for our review with Peter."

The next half-hour was spent with the two people looking though their respective surveys and identifying those areas they had scored the same and those that they had scored differently.

It was clear they did a good job with sales.

However when it came to providing research support, this area was weak. They did not really seem to know about the competition other than the usual stuff that Sales had collected at trade shows or in discussions with customers.

Sarah scored the product development area lower than Adam. It was becoming clear they needed to get a better perspective on this business technique of marketing.

They summarized what they had learned and ended the meeting by agreeing that the next meeting with the three of them, should start to help build on this new learning.

4

They met at Adam's office on Friday. He walked in just a few minutes late, having run over at his last meeting. "Sorry I am late. I hope you got everything you need Peter?"

Peter said "Yes, warm Coke Cola no ice is just what I need this time in the afternoon." Sarah had her usual coffee mug and Adam grabbed a quick hot tea.

"Well Peter, here are the surveys we did and the results we got. We scored a 7 or 8. These are the areas we are strong on but these are the things we are weak on."

Peter said, "And what do you think you need to do now?"

Adam said, "Well I really want to know more about what Marketing is, but I want to know what it is going to give the company before I spend a lot of time working on it."

"Let's start there." Peter replied "Marketing is one of those things that when I was in Sales I thought I was doing a lot of and then, as I started working in the Marketing area I began to understand what Marketing was all about. It became a lot clearer, it is really a group of business techniques and tools to create increased revenues and profits. Now I know that sounds like every other thing we are supposed to do in business, but it really is what the goal of Marketing is for a business."

"For example, when we were looking to expand the Canadian box chocolate business we would have gone to the United States as our expansion market. Using marketing surveys and analysis we learned that chocolate consumption was declining in the U.S. but growing in the Asian markets. So we focused in that area first. The impact on the sales revenue was significant. We were glad we selected a market with stronger options to enter, to fund our entry later into the US."

"Let's spend the time today just thinking about why we need Marketing or a different type of Marketing at CONE Inc. You have said the number of products in your company has grown. Is that correct?"

Adam replied, "Absolutely. What the company started with eight years ago is completely different from what we have today. We still have the first product and we still sell a few of them, but we have created a lot of other products and we have even bought a couple of products. Also, we have added services to the business mix."

"Okay. What do you know about your competition?" asked Peter.

"Oh, we know a lot about them. We go to trade shows and pick up their literature and promotional materials." Stated Adam. "What about the pricing area Sarah?"

Sarah said, "Yes, we get some of their price lists and we look closely at them. Then we put together some key business graphs and charts. I think the sales guys know what is going on with their competition."

Peter then asked, "I would like to know who manages the various products or product lines?"

To which Adam replied, "Well, we all do. Sales gives us some good input and R&D comes up with stuff. We have management meetings in which we get into the act and provide some items and direction. Sometimes manufacturing seems a little confused. They tell us there are too many people telling them what to do, but they work hard and they always come up with the answers in the end."

Peter again asked, "How often do you talk to your customers?"

"Good question," said Adam,"we don't spend a lot of time talking to our customers about our products or services. We sell our customers. We know what they really need and we can get in there and sell them what we make."

"OK that is a start. I am beginning to get a clearer picture of the current situation. How do you set your CONE Inc. Marketing budget or budgets?" asked Peter.

"Well, the Marketing budget is sort of whatever the guys need. You know, if the sales guys say we need trade shows then it's trade shows. If they say we need brochures or updated brochures, we go off and have them printed. Whatever we need to keep the business rolling along."

Next Peter asked, " So, do you do strategic planning or business planning?"

"Oh yes," answered Sarah, "every year we go off site from the office and spend two days identifying all the things that are issues and opportunities and challenges. We write them all down and our people get all sorts of tasks out of it. We do have strategic planning."

"We even had a consultant come in and help us the first year, set up how we should do it. One of the key things we learned was' Although strategic planning may seem a sterile, intellectual analytical process, it's not. As … the human element is critical important." (2)

Peter then queried, "How do you manage your products as part of that strategic planning process?"

"Well the strategic planning really has to do with the whole business unit, we never look at just individual products or groups of products," said Adam.

"Let me sow a seed here for you to think on." Stated Peter. "Do you think the large companies like IBM, General Electric or Ralston Purina do strategic planing for just the company or do they look at the company and individual products? Let's not spend time to-day discussing this but think about this for one of the next meetings."

Peter then said, "What I think we really need to get a grip on are the benefits of Marketing so you can see that it can do a number of things for you and CONE Inc.. Let me start off by reviewing what you have just said, but change it from a Marketing perspective.

"Adam when we talk about Marketing, one of the things you said was - 'the company started eight years ago with one product and now you have a bunch of products and services'. From Marketing's point of view, we need to do some portfolio management to group-like products."

"This will help us to find out what products we should keep, which ones we should support, which ones we should cut. We need to have the same technique for the services"

"Now do not get too concerned with some of the concepts or phrases I am setting out. We will explore a number of them later. Right now we just need to get a better grasp on this marketing thing from a broad perspective. I like to call it the 30,000 foot level look. We can see all the parts of the landscape, but not the ants crawling around,' commented Peter.

"You mentioned that you pick up things from trade shows, literature and promotions. But if we had a formal method or process of analyzing competitors strengths and weaknesses then we could look at each competitor on an equal basis. This would allow you to analyze them from a Marketing point of view. All their key products and services and their relative positions in the various markets."

Sarah said, "Don't forget those price lists. We look at those and we put together some charts and stuff for the sales people to look at the regional meetings. We really know our pricing."

"But the real thing is not just pricing," said Peter. "It's a number of things that go together, along with pricing, to add value to CONE Inc. products. Things such as product or packaging, but as I said before this is the 30,000-foot look before we cover the details and techniques of Marketing. "

"Customers don't buy on price. Now let's not get too concerned about that statement," said Peter quickly. "But remember it and when we get to talk about pricing, you will understand what I mean."

Peter looked at Adam with a smile, "Do you need another tea or shall we just carry on?"

"No, no this is getting interesting," replied Adam quickly. "Please carry on converting what we talked about into Marketing language or Marketing thoughts."

Peter said, "You talked about R&D coming up with stuff, well what we need to do is provide them some direction, and that is what Marketing must do."

"Marketing identifies what customer needs are, what the long-term trends are and really provides them some development parameters based on that analysis."

"But, and it is a big but," stated Adam "that is exactly the kind of thing which cuts down creativity. When the R&D guys are told exactly what to do, that is what they will deliver! No more no less, they really feel stifled."

Peter added, "Marketing really is providing parameters, not putting blindfolds on or creating things so tight people won't know where to go. Providing parameters assists people to focus or direct their creative thinking."

"We really need to define Marketing, and that is what we are going to do shortly." Finished Peter.

"Do you have a sense of why we need Marketing yet? Or is it still kind of a gray area?" he asked.

Sarah quickly said, "I am getting the sense of it, but you know it is still kind of gray. I think we need to think of a definition of Marketing and really create a foundation that we can build from for other Marketing items."

Adam smiled (Sarah is not just a numbers person) he thought. Then he said out loud, "You're right, we really needed to have the definition. I would like to spend a little bit of time thinking about it though. Perhaps we can meet in a week or so and create a definition."

"Great," said Peter "how about 2:00 p.m. next Thursday? I've got an afternoon free and we could spend some time coming up with the definition. However, before we come up with the definition I would like to give you a little work to think about between now and our next meeting. I would like you to think about why Marketing is really needed.

"Once we understand that, it will help us in terms of creating the definition which fits your company and it's needs."

With that, Adam and Sarah walked out feeling a little better knowing they were now getting some understanding.

But they were still a little concerned because they didn't seem to be making great progress.

"Do you think it is going a little slow?" Sarah asked Adam. She was concerned this seemed to be taking longer than she had hope for to find directions and key items to action.

"Not really," commented Adam, " you know it's taken eight years to this point. It is going to take us more than one or two meetings to sort it out and make sure we have got the right direction."

Adam looked at Sarah and could tell by the look on her face that she was deep in thought. She needed to see the next step to this project. Not just the next meeting but perhaps some discussion time.

"What we want to do is perhaps meet on Thursday, in your office, and spend some time putting together 'Why we feel we need Marketing at CONE Inc.', and we can round out some key thoughts and points before we come back and meet with Peter. I will e-mail you some optional times and look forward to hearing from you."

"Don't worry Sarah, there is an answer here somewhere."
laughed Adam, as they arrived at their cars.

Adam really felt ready for dinner. 'We really have started to
cover a lot of ground in this new Marketing business area.'
Was his last thought as he turned his car onto the street from
the company parking lot and headed for home.

Sarah smiled as she followed Adam's car onto the street.
'Yes it was time for dinner' she thought.

5

Adam got up from behind his desk and picked up his file. He had done some work during the weekend and added a couple of notes on Monday and Tuesday about why he thought Marketing was really needed. He was looking forward to the meeting in the next hour with Sarah, just to review where they were at, and to get a feeling for it. He also realized he should get other people's opinions in the company, but he wanted to get a better handle on where they were going before he did that.

When he entered meeting room 4C, Sarah was already there with her coffee and a hot tea for him.

"Well Sarah," he said, "did you get a chance to do some thinking and write out any notes?"

"Of course I did," Sarah replied impatiently. "This is an important project and I am really enjoying working on it. But we do need to put some time into it, you are right about that."

"What I would like to do is review our notes and then we can put them on the flip chart."

After an hour, they had come to a mutual agreement and added some key points to each others thoughts.

"I am beginning to get a real feel that Marketing is much more complicated than I originally thought," commented Sarah with the little frown she had when deep in thought.

"You are right," said Adam, " but I am beginning to understand there are reasons why Marketing is really growing in importance, and I am looking forward to meeting with Peter tomorrow."

6

The next day was sunny and bright as they drove to the university for their meeting with Peter. They were both beginning to feel better about Marketing, and believed they were really starting to get some insights into it, as a business discipline needed at CONE Inc.

They knocked at the door and walked into Peter's office. They sat down in their customary chairs around the table in the corner. The sun shone in and lit up their spirits as well as the room.

"Well," said Peter when he met them, "did you make a list of why you think Marketing is important?"

"Yes," both Sarah and Adam said quickly together and then they laughed. This was getting to be fun.

"Let's review some of those points," continued Peter "Then we can understand exactly what we need to build on, or if you are doing fine with understanding why Marketing is needed and we can start to delve into the various marketing areas."

Adam started by saying, "what we would like to do is go through each of our concepts or ideas, and discuss each so we all understand them the same way. Does that make sense Peter?"

Peter agreed. "Really I need to understand where you are so I can help you build on that. By having a common understanding we can set the core elements up and build on that foundation."

"For a start," Adam said, "we realize there are a lot of people doing just functional tasks in the CONE company. R&D is doing its function, Sales is doing its function, Manufacturing is doing its function, Finance is doing its function."

"Everyone is carrying out a job or company function and while they may be just related to the job function before and after, there is no real thread or overall picture. If senior management do not share the overall picture or perspective on the project we don't see opportunities to add value or create value or generate business-building ideas. Plus we are only internally focused rather then looking at the marketplace trends"

"Very good," commented Peter, "you have identified one of the key things. Everybody in their own job function area may be performing very well. However, the Marketing function must be integrated, thereby linking all those other functions on a day to day or project by project basis."

"So," said Sarah, "Marketing is really a function, but it is kind of like a management function. It is an overview linking many business things."

"That's right," said Peter, "However, Marketing is a different function than Senior Management. Senior Management is providing direction for the whole company, right?"

"Yes" answered Adam "That is our job and the executive committee's responsibility."

"Okay," followed Peter, "But Marketing's responsibility is to understand the market place and the individual product needs and functions. So they are down a layer, not looking where the company as a whole is going, but where each product or product group is going."

"From a decision making point of view," Sarah interjected, "what we are finding is that we make a lot of decisions internally and develop things, products or services and provide them to the customers."

Sarah continued, " We think if we had a Marketing orientation, we would tend to look at what the customer needs are and provide products or services based on their focus and needs."

Peter said, "Yes, if you really look at it from an economic point of view, the decision making by Marketing tends to get into the whole area of not just profits but social responsibility, economics, and several other key macro areas. [3] Marketing is concerned with the whole customer group, rather than with just one individual customer."

"Exactly," said Adam, "and that is one of the key areas for Sales. We have a key account Sales group and they are really focused on their specific individual customers or accounts."

"However, sometimes I think we miss an opportunity because there isn't somebody saying, 'if it's good for these two accounts, how many other accounts like that are there'?"

"Exactly right," answered Peter. "But right now we are getting a little too focused in the details of the company. The question I gave you to think about was 'Why is Marketing growing in importance'?"

Adam added, "Another thing we noticed is there is a slowing of real growth in the marketplace."

Peter exclaimed, "That's correct."

"Unless you are in those leading edge markets," Adam continued, "there seems to be a real slowing of the overall economy. In fact, many forecasters estimate the growth in business volume at 2% to3%, productivity gains at 2% to 3%, and inflation between 2% and 3%."

Peter again confirmed the statements, saying, "That's right, we no longer have economics driven on a regional or national basis because of world wars or other factors. We are now growth driven in terms of market needs."

"What are some of the other things that you noted?" continued Peter.

Sarah jumped in, "Well one of the things we have noted, especially in accounting, is that technology is changing significantly."

"We also noted it in other parts of the company, from manufacturing to R&D and really what the customer wants are for our products." Continued Sarah.

"Yes," said Peter, "what you're seeing is technology impacting what you're manufacturing, what you are creating and what the needs are of your clients. For example, look at this computer. If you were at the college ten years ago, we weren't looking at using computers. And they only occasionally used videos in class. Now we have satellite links to students who can't come to class. What else have you noted?"

"Well," continued Adam, "I have noticed that deregulation is impacting some of the areas we are looking at for CONE. Certain markets that were regulated by Governments are being deregulated, creating competition and changing the whole marketplace."

"Another good observation," Peter commented. "Yes, deregulation means we have competition, and competition is one of the things Marketing must handle."

"That's not to say Marketing is the only function in the company that handles or looks at competitors. But it is one of the elements people in the Marketing function must handle."

Sarah noted also, "Life style changes have created new markets and changed existing markets significantly. If we look at the fitness market, eating habits, things like bottled water. Bottled water! Wow things have really changed."

"Overall the baby boomers have changed the way we look at markets and their wants and needs are significantly different than those of generations before. One of the things these newer generations accept more is change. They accept it and are comfortable with change."

Peter again continued, "The other thing you will note is in organizations where Marketing becomes a specific function, the walls tend to come down between areas, as all functions work together to meet the customer's needs."

Adam jumped in, "Wait a minute! We have that now. We are all working toward the customer's need."

"Yes, I agree," said Sarah, "we are all working towards that customer need."

Peter jumped in, "Let me ask you a question. Do each of the functions work together or do each of the functions work for and toward the customer?"

Adam answered "Well they, um, they tend to focus on the customer."

"But do they work together?" questioned Peter.

"Hum, good question." pondered Adam. "Overall I guess we still work by department, but they are specialized departments. The total effort isn't really guided by what the customer wants, but by what we think we can give the customer. Hum, I'm starting to see a picture forming here."

"One of the other things we mentioned earlier today," Peter continued, "was competition. If we look back to the early 50's and 60's, there may not have been much competition, or when you developed your first product in your company, you may not have had much competition for it."

"But as CONE Inc. developed, other people came onto the market with similar and competitive products or services, correct?"

"Yes" said Adam, "We seem to be generating more and more competition. Why, it seems every time we create new products or develop new services, some other new and different company we haven't seen before comes at us!"

Sarah joined in at this point, "Yes, it is kind of confusing sometimes with all the competitors out there just trying to keep track of them."

Peter jumped back in, "Yes, and this is why we look at having a business function that can manage that on a focused basis. You have to understand the competition from the controllable elements and the uncontrollable elements. Most of the time we simply focus on controllable elements."

"Just so we are all talking from the same perspective let me clarify my statement on the controllable elements and the uncontrollable elements. This is an important core concept to understand when thinking about what is Marketing."

"The uncontrollable elements are those external factors. Let me give you a few examples that will help to set up the concept."

"One example is Governments. When there is a change in the government and the new one has different priorities that means new legislation."

"The weather is another uncontrollable. If you have a snow storm then JIT deliveries can be slowed up shutting down production, or a late frost can kill a farmers crops. An other uncontrollable is the social environment. We just have to look at the whole area of greening to see the impact of this element on business. One big factor we have covered is the competitive environment. One company buys another company. Or a company develops a new to the world product or service and the entire marketplace changes."

"The controllable elements are those that are internal. They: are the product, pricing, promotion and place or distribution."

"So," continued Peter quietly from his chair, " if I was to summarize, would you now agree that Marketing is a more important function than you thought before, and it seems to be growing in importance as a business technique?"

Adam answered, "Yes, I think you are right. I think we have not really understood this Marketing and what it was supposed to accomplish, therefore, I don't know we give it the support needed."

"What we need to do," said Peter, "is to understand more of the benefits of Marketing, and then we can create a definition. Let me do some work and the next time we get together, next week, we can go through what I believe are the key benefits of Marketing. Then we can create that all important Marketing definition for CONE Inc."

They established a time for the next meeting and Adam left.

Sarah turned to Peter and said, "This seems to be taking a long time. Is there anyway we could do this faster?"

"Sarah," said Peter, "I really wanted to get thinking in the right mode. Maybe we could do several meetings in one week now that we have generated some basic understanding."

Back at his office Adam pulled a green three ring binder out of his desk drawer and set up lined pages inside. 'I want to start capturing some of these key concepts on paper so I can review them as we move along.' he thought.

For his first notes he wrote

At CONE Inc. everyone is carrying out a function. They may only look at the function before and after their function.

Marketing looks at all the internal company functions and can unify them with an overall perspective, breaking down the current department or team barriers.

So a CONE business model currently would look like:

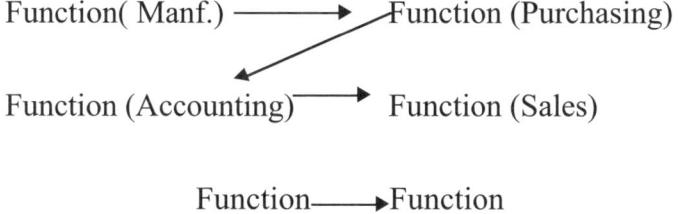

Function(Manf.) ⟶ Function (Purchasing)

Function (Accounting) ⟶ Function (Sales)

Function⟶Function

CONE Inc. could, with Marketing, look like this:

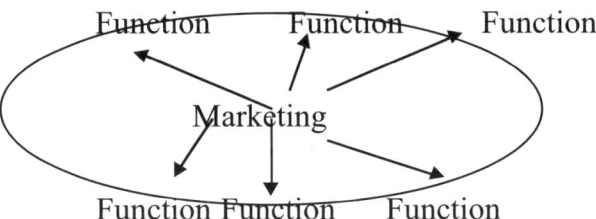

Function   Function   Function

Marketing

Function Function   Function

This was a great start to the many notes and ideas to come.
He closed the green binder and felt as if he was beginning to
see the concept of Marketing more clearly now.

7

After dinner Peter sat down in his den and thought about the meeting yesterday with Sarah and Adam.

I really need to start moving this project along, but at the same time I do not want to move so fast that I lose them.

He had looked up several definitions of Marketing and decided to build toward one he had used for several years.

'I do not want to get too academic with this definition' he thought, 'but it is very important to have a clear definition of Marketing.'

The definition will become the springboard for moving the process of understanding Marketing forward. It must not be so narrow it limits the use, or too broad that it is not functional.

Looking around the den he thought, ' I need to think of a product and then outline it. Yes that will work."

Thinking back to dinner he remembered the great salad. Maybe lettuce? No, something more basic. How about the great warm bread they had. Yes, bread the staff of life!

If they were to focus on bread from a Marketing perspective they would have to know how many people use bread?

How do they use it - for snacks, toast, fish bait or other uses? Did they want sliced or unsliced?

What price would they pay for white, whole wheat or raisin bread?

Would they pay more for bread that was hand baked, special style, or were ingredients the key?

Packaging is another item. How did they want to see it packaged? In a plastic bag, brown paper wrap, or cloth?

Distribution was another area. Where did they expect to buy their bread? Would they look for it in specialty shops? How else could one distribute bread?

All these items are what people want and have little to do with what the baker can make or wants. If the baker was the greatest animal shape bread baker in the world it didn't matter if no one wanted alligator shaped bread.

Then Peter wrote down a long list of key benefits of Marketing he could use later in the meeting with Sarah and Adam.

He felt it would be important for providing direction to the exploration of the key benefits of the business tool of Marketing.

He finished his tea and leaned back in his chair, time to stop work and go watch a classic video with his wife, just time to relax overall and stop thinking about Marketing.

He looked around his den and was glad he had spent time at home gathering his thoughts.

'Sometimes we just take for granted why we do Marketing.' He thought. 'It was interesting to revisit the basics and look at them from a business building point of view.

As he left the den he looked at the CONE Inc. Marketing file on his desk. It was getting thicker after each key meeting with Sarah and Peter. This is really fun he thought!

8

When they met early the next week, Sarah shared with Adam that she was trying to move the process ahead a little faster. Realizing that it would take some time to create the functions at CONE, plus the techniques and tools they needed, she was eager to move to a level where they could start.

They had set this meeting at CONE Inc. The meeting room was one of the many conference rooms. It had a flip chart and some notes on the conference room white board, Adam had made for discussion.

Peter started the conversation by saying, "I want you to make sure you understand the benefit of Marketing products or groups of products and services. If you agree on that, then we can create a definition of Marketing for CONE Inc. When we meet later in the week we can start breaking out 'How Marketing has been successful for various products.' with examples."

"One of the reasons we want to pull products or groups of products together and market them is that it generates some efficiencies."

"Efficiencies come various ways. Advertising creative can be used in several places, such as magazines, posters and trade show materials. Media discounts are available for multiple pages in the same magazine or newspaper. Production print runs of catalogues or trade show literature for several products can be ganged together to get discounts compared to running them separately. Promotional programs for several products can be set up simultaneously to get premium discounts."

"By tying together several products we can make the costs lower on a per product basis. Just like we would if we looked at the per unit cost of raw materials in production. Would you agree with that?" questioned Peter. "This is the first real benefit."

Sarah and Adam both nodded and Sarah answered, "Yes that makes sense."

"Another major benefit is Marketing's research and understanding exactly what the customer's wants and needs are, and matching that to the trends in the marketplace. For example, if you were to create a product for a leading edge Hi tech industry right now, you would probably not make it a DOS only product. However, if you were to create a product for the Government or a third world country, a DOS base product might be exactly what they want, or could use, depending on their type of computers. Only research for the broad market can really tell you what to do."

"So, one of the benefits is, Marketing can define what the real customer wants and needs are and what the marketplace real needs are," stated Sarah in a matter of fact way.

'This would improve our new product success rate,' she thought to herself. 'we would be launching products that had a real need in the market, not just what we can make.'

"Okay" said Adam, "I think I have seen some benefits, but there must be more?"

"Yes," replied Peter. "Let me give you a couple more. Marketing can manage the whole pricing area, by not only looking at competition, but at what the internal costs are. Both are important elements to analyze when setting pricing."

"Is it fair to say that Sales knows what competitors pricing is for a given product or service?" asked Peter.

"Yes," said Sarah, "that's one of the areas we are very proud of at CONE Inc."

"However," continued Peter, "does Sales know what the actual internal costs are to create the product or service?"

Sarah replied, "Well they don't know the exact cost or the breakdown, but they know what our final cost is and the company markup."

"Correct," said Peter. "However, based on that philosophy we really need someone who can dig in and tear apart all the product or service costs. If we are to increase efficiencies, or if we go in a new product direction, or any number of things that can impact the product and thus affect the revenue. Costs to manufacture or the profit that we make off of it, we need that person who can look at all the areas."

"As you may have noticed in the car industry, they have a technique called de-contenting. This is where the auto industry has reduced some of the content of the car to reduce the price to customers. For example the 1997 Ford Taurus trimmed $180 off the cost of each car by doing a number of things. The splash shields under the wheel wells used recycled plastic rather than new plastic, saving 45 cents. Engineers borrowed a part from another Ford model to reinforce the sheet metal under the seat for savings of $1.50. They could only do this by knowing all the costs of all the parts"

"Why do this? Competitive levels of pricing from off-shore cars, continue to put pressure, driving pricing down for cars rather than automatically increasing the list price."

"Another key benefit is that we have someone or some group that is focused solely on the individual product or group of products or service. It means they are looking after the health of that particular product and all the various elements. Just like the mission statement drives the company, these people can take the product and drive that product with certain Marketing tools." Peter took a breath.

"I think we are starting to have a good feel for this," said Adam, "but I would still like to set a definition of Marketing."

"Well," said Peter, "what we normally do is work with the total company to do that, but since you two are representing it at the moment, let's put together a working definition which we can then use as we move forward on this project."

"As with any definition, it is something you start with and build from. It must help us understand what Marketing is and how it can be a useful business technique. It must be clear for all the people at CONE Inc. It really becomes the mission statement for the Marketing effort."

"The definition I would like to suggest is -

Marketing is the management and development of a business activities through analysis, making decisions, and executing programs to satisfy present and potential customers and company needs, while generating profitable revenues, within corporate guidelines. " © (4)

"If we break this down, we can see that we are going to start with analysis; we are going to understand what the customer wants and needs are; we are going to understand what the marketplace is; and we are going to do a number of reviews to understand how to manage and develop the business."

"We are going to make fact based decisions. This means we are not only going to do the analysis, but we are going to make decisions and provide suggestions and actionable recommendations. Executing programs means once we have presented our material to management or other departments, we are going create programs that will use that information. We are trying to satisfy the customer needs. This is important."

"I like that definition," commented Adam. "It will add to our company, to our planning and to our overall management process."

As he took a sip of his hot tea he added, "I now begin to understand more of where Marketing fits in the company and what it is really supposed to do."

Sarah added, "Yes, I am beginning to see now that it is an overall framework for the Marketing process to integrate into the company."

"One of the other things to note," said Peter, "is Marketing, like any business discipline, has its own terminology and techniques that are the tools to help create the Marketing materials and programs."

"As we noted in the definition," he continued, "Marketing works with functional groups inside the company and outside suppliers or partners, to find ways of meeting the customer needs and expectations and develop new parts to the product to exceed their needs and expectations. That is all part of what they are going to do."

"Great! Well that is another building block," said Adam, "in this overall process."

"Just a quick question before we go." Sarah turned to Peter again, "Does this mean that we want to satisfy all the customer needs all of the time?"

"Good question," answered Peter, "No! But when the firm focuses it's efforts on satisfying some customer needs, it will create a larger business opportunity than if it just focused on what the business can produce. It creates a better selling opportunity, a better opportunity for repeat sales, a better opportunity to keep people sold, and a better opportunity for more satisfied customers. "

"Before we leave these topics, I think we should identify some key companies where Marketing has been extremely successful in driving it forward."

"If we look at Intel, they have used Marketing to establish a presence and a leadership for a product very few people see, but many people know. The computer chip. They have done an excellent job of using all the Marketing mix elements (Price, Place, Promotion and Product) to support Intel."

" In fact Intel used many of the Marketing tools the majority of their competitors didn't think about, until they did it first. Subsequently they have a huge share of the market at about 90%+ on a Global bases, as of mid-1998."

"Southwest Airlines," Peter continued, "started with strategic planning, used promotion, and pricing heavily to establish themselves. Along with a unique position in a small segment of the air travel marketplace."

"Equally important they continue to follow their founding strategy. For example in the Baltimore/ Washington to Providence route Southwest picked up 74% of all passengers, with US Airways having the rest. They do this by having one way fares of $38 to $62 compared to competitors one way fares at $138 to $ 189 (in earlier 1998)." Noted Peter.

"Through successful Marketing South West Airlines have been continuously profitable every quarter since they were launched. They are the only airline in North America that has that profit record, and one of the few in the world."

"If we look at the 'not for profit' area, the United Way has done an excellent job of Marketing its service across North America and establishing itself as one of the driving forces in the whole charity area. As well, they have been successful in meeting their goals and exceeding those goals for many years, through extremely effective Marketing, promotion and funneling of a sales force that is made up of volunteers."

"Now," said Peter, " these are all big companies. But Marketing is for all sizes of companies. It really has to do with the life cycle of company growth. As companies start up they have one product and a small base or set of customers using their products and services. They usually do not have competitors since they are first to the marketplace with a new product or service."

"As companies move along the company life cycle and create multiple products, multiple services, various competitions and many customers, Marketing needs to be a part of how they do business. Marketing needs to focus the efforts to increase sales revenue and profitability."

"Those are great," said Adam. "The more I think about it, the more I see that highly successful companies are ones that use Marketing effectively. Well Sarah, this is definitely something we have to keep looking at."

"I think what we have to do," added Peter, "is look at how Marketing has been successful for products and services. If we could do that later this week, it would give you more parts of the overall Marketing puzzle, in terms of understanding this whole thing."

Adam went back to his office. He wanted to get these new Marketing thoughts and items down. As he sat in his office chair he began to think of all the new learning that he was gaining in this key project.

He gazed out the window and his mind started to think of the impact Marketing must have had on the business world. 'Wow, it is a bigger business discipline than I had suspected. Well to the project at hand'

Adam opened his green Marketing binder and wrote down the definition of Marketing that had been on the flip chart.

Marketing is the management and development of a business through analysis, making decisions, and executing programs to satisfy the company needs, while generating profitable revenues, within corporate guidelines. [©]

Next he listed some of the benefits.

To pull products or groups of products together and market them in such a way as to generate some efficiencies.

Marketing can define what the real customer wants and needs are, and what the marketplace can provide or is providing.

Marketing can manage the whole pricing area, by looking at not only at the competition, but at what internal costs are as well as customer pricing expectations.

We need to have someone or some group that is focused solely on the individual product or group of like products.

Highly successful companies are ones that have used Marketing very effectively.

Highly successful companies continue to use Marketing every day.

Yes, there were some key management items here to help build the CONE Inc. company to the next level!

9

Three days later they met again at the CONE Inc. offices. This time it was in a conference room with several flip charts so they could capture all the ideas. Peter had been given his own security pass and he felt like one of the CONE company members.

"It's interesting," began Peter, "as I was walking up here, I saw all those pine cones laying on the ground. It helped me understand why you ended up calling this CONE Inc."

Adam laughed, "Yes, it was one of the factors that helped name it when we started up in this location."

They gathered around a table and each had their usual beverages, Adam with his tea, Sarah with her coffee, and Peter with his warm Coke Cola. They were relaxed, but with a certain amount of excitement between Sarah and Adam as they were beginning to understand more about this Marketing discipline. They were looking forward to discussing those elements that Peter had called the Marketing Mix.

They understood the Marketing Mix was: Product; Price; Place and Promotion and they wanted to know how Marketing really looked at those elements.

Peter began, "Adam, can you tell me what a product is and what it is made of?"

"Sure," answered Adam, "it's, ah, you know, it's, ah, it's got ridges and ruffles and colours and a price tag, and Big C service behind it and . . . ."

"Wait a minute," interrupted Peter, "but if you were to summarize all those, what are they?"

Adam added, "They are the features and benefits."

"Exactly," said Peter. "A product is composed of features and benefits that, when delivered to the customer, meet a set of their needs or wants. [5] The other thing we have to remember is product features are both tangible and intangible."

"An intangible feature," said Sarah, "what does that mean?"

Peter continued. "Tangible is something that I can touch and feel and see and smell or taste. Intangible are those things that come with the product. For example: when I sit here drinking Coca Cola, Coca Cola comes with an intangible feeling that is created by the brand name, all the advertising and all the history behind it. All the intangible emotion, feeling and image that comes through."

So Adam said, "Help me understand again why Marketing is important for products."

Peter went to the easel and drew a bell curve. He turned and said, "This is a technique called the Life Cycle. Every product moves through it. Someone has to manage it at each stage of the cycle. They need to understand where each product is in that curve, so they know exactly what to do in terms of strategy."

"Some products move through it faster than others. The 'Pet Rock', or the Tamagotchis cyber pets, for example probably moved through it in 90 days. If we were to think of some leading edge products such as the main frame computer, has it gone through it's life cycle yet? No. It is still moving through it. Coca Cola is maybe at the top of the bell but it certainly isn't in decline."

"The area of electronic games, some of them have certainly gone through the cycle, but the overall concept of electronic games continues to get newer and better products entering at the beginning of the bell and moving their way through the bell curve or life cycle curve."

"Someone has to manage this, and not just on a client by client basis. In the long-term this is where Marketing can be successful. It can identify where the product is on the bell curve; it can identify what are the things we should be doing (or strategies as we call them); it can identify the key objectives that must be used to increase the volumes."

"Remember back to the definition where we said 'analyze', well that's one of the things Marketing can do. It must analyze the products from a customer perspective and a business perspective."

Peter thought for a moment and then began. " Let me give you an example. The Edsel was the most researched car ever created by Ford in the early fifties. But it did not work. Why? Well it took seven years to move from original research to the market. Remember this was the early fifties. In the late forties when the car concept was researched, people were just getting over the war. They wanted the best and money was not an issue. But in the mid-fifties they had begun life in the family mode. They moved to the suburbs and had kids. Now they wanted an economical and a family car. The style appeals changed for the car design. The Edsel was premium priced with low gas mileage and lots of chrome. Now take the Mustang, it moved from consumer research to the public in fewer years and it gave them what they wanted, a sports car with power but not so much that mom or dad or the kids could not drive it."

" Marketing can also group products together and look at segmenting the market or creating groups of products in the marketplace. Like compact cars or luxury cars for example" remarked Peter.

"Wait a minute," said Adam "this is a lot of information. What's this segmenting of products? Does it come before or after product development?"

"If you think about various changes in demographics and we take a particular product, what are the needs of those people. For example the car: if you are single; in your early 20's - you're looking for economy; sportiness; image; a whole number of things. But if you are 35 years old, married with 2 kids and a mortgage - you need a family vehicle (different than when you were 21 when you were still in school or had your first job).

" To answer your other question, segmentation starts before product or service development. It is one of the marketing techniques that help to focus information in identifying the real needs of the customer.

"One of the other things," Peter added, "which is extremely important for Marketing to do, is to develop the product positioning. It is really a key statement for managing the Marketing of any product successfully"

"Positioning sets out why the customer should buy the product, it is really the Mission Statement of the product. Just like the Mission Statement driving the company, the Product Positioning Statement drives the product or product groups. We can have a Service Positioning Statement for services as well."

Sarah said, "Wait a minute. This seems to be fairly complicated in developing a whole bunch of positioning statements."

Peter looked at her, took a sip of his Coca Cola and formed some thoughts in his mind. Then he remarked, "It is complicated, that is one of the reasons why Marketing must take control of it. However, Marketing needs a lot of input to develop the Positioning Statement. Information can be generated by people internally about the product features and benefits and what it can do, what it can't do."

"Externally, Marketing can look at competition, it can do research with customers and the Sales force to find out what they are looking for and what they will accept. It is one of those tools that can be complicated, but it is extremely important and is one of the reasons why Marketing must drive it forward."

"You had asked us," Sarah followed, "to break down all the things or elements in a product, and I was surprised by the long list I had actually developed. When I started looking at a product like a TV, I said 'well there is the physical product, there is the service support, there are the features, there is the quality level, there is the warranty, there are the colours, there is the style, there is the name, and there is the price, there are a lot of different elements."

"That's good," suggested Peter, "but what you are doing is identifying a whole list of elements that have to be managed by someone."

"If you multiply that by the number of products you have, you start to see the complexity of it."

"Really it can't be managed just by Research & Development, or Manufacturing, or Senior Management, it requires the focus of an individual, a product manager or brand champion to integrate all the elements."

"When we look at the industrial side," remarked Adam, "I guess there is also the things such as raw materials, components, maintenance, supplies, repairs, all those elements that go into making up a product or service."

"Exactly," said Peter, "Now you are beginning to get the understanding of why these things called products and services, are complex and need someone to manage them that has a good picture of both the internal and external elements."

"Also, we have to understand how industrial products or business to business products, are different from consumer products in that industrial products usually have a driven demand. Like we need toilet paper in the washrooms at the office or writing paper at the office or floppy discs for computers."

"Whereas, consumer products can be impulse in nature. Like getting gum or a magazine when you buy milk."

"Price increases in the industrial area may slow down or speed up how products are used. We will talk more about pricing in the next couple of days."

"Tax treatments and laws are also different," said Sarah, "A capital item is a long lasting product that can be used and depreciated over many years. It can be very expensive when it is first purchased and therefore, replacing it can be a long cycle."

"Yes," added Adam "that is one of the things we have incurred with the Acme mobile item. While many people wanted it and we got good initial purchase, the product has a life cycle of about 8 years."

"Since it was only introduced 2 years ago, we are still working through the cycle of first purchases rather than replacements."

"I think that is all we can take for today," interjected Adam. "Thanks Peter, we look forward to our meeting in two days, when we are going to talk about distribution."

As he got to his office, Sarah asked, " What is your hurry?"

"I want to get my summary notes into my green binder before I forget all of them," Adam stated.

"I might have known," laughed Sarah, "You would start to keep notes. This means you are starting to see long term value here. Great! I feel the same way. I had not really set up a formal set of notes but I had the feeling you might."

As he opened the green Marketing book he wrote

Marketing Mix is Product, Place, Price and Promotion

All of these elements are part of how you do Marketing.

A product is composed of features and benefits that when delivered to the customer, meets a set of needs or wants.

Someone has to manage the product or service life cycle.

Marketing can group like products using segmentation.

Positioning is the mission statement of the product.

There is a variety of elements to this Marketing area. He was really starting to see the complexity but the logic in how it could be used for business. More importantly how CONE Inc. could integrate marketing into their business.

Closing the binder he turned and looked out the window. He could see the sun was getting low in the western sky.

Time to go home and barbecue up a dinner for the family. Yes, a nice barbecued steak and a Bette special salad would just hit the hunger spot.

With that he laughed and headed for the parking lot.

10

Several days later they met at the CONE offices. It was early in the morning and Sarah made sure there was plenty of coffee and hot tea. Adam had stopped and brought in muffins and croissants. They needed to spend a couple of hours before the day started, but this Marketing project was becoming very important.

Peter started the meeting by saying, "We need to focus on this whole area of Distribution, or Place. During the 1980's Compaq computers grew faster than any other company in the history of computers."

" Why? Because they took advantage of market growth quickly, introducing new models of personal computers for market segments Compaq saw neglected by IBM and other companies. It has worked extremely well for them, as they quickly dominated several segments of the PC market not only in the United States, but also in international markets."

He continued with another example, "If we think of DELL computers, they have no retail outlets and yet have generated billions of dollars in sales. How have they done that? Initially by using a channel of distribution called Telephone or TeleMarketing or Direct sales."

"All right," said Adam, "that's interesting but how can Marketing really help make us more successful in this whole area of Distribution?"

Peter looked at them and said, "We have to understand that we need someone who is going to manage the process of distribution. We have to know what the ideal places are for a particular product, what is the sales force role, and we have to understand if middlemen are a benefit or not."

"Wait a minute," interrupted Sarah, "What do you mean by middlemen?"

"Middlemen are those distributors, wholesalers, agents or brokers that handle your products in various areas, not only in America or Canada, but also Internationally," answered Peter. "It may be more effective to use a broker or agent who can get into key accounts with our products and carry it as one of the products they carry, rather than trying to set up an independent CONE Inc. sales force."

"What! Wait a second," exclaimed Adam, "this is going into a lot of theory. How will I know this is really important and Marketing should handle it?"

"Well it goes back to understanding the target audience and competition." commented Peter. "When we understand where the people will go to get a product. Or what incentives would get them to go to a certain place. Whether the competition is selling in certain locations, then we can plan where to get our distribution and get it in the most effective place possible."

"We are trying to be the most efficient and make the best use of our dollars wherever possible, and Marketing's challenge is to find that and demonstrate it in a planned, fact based and controlled sense."

"One of the things Marketing must do is decide the characteristics of the distribution channel. In other words they need to do segmentation, to decide what are the characteristics (direct, do we need middlemen, or how else could it be done) and the type of channel. For example the Franklin Mint sells direct to customers, Belair Insurance or Travellers Insurance sell straight to people not using Brokers or a middleman."

"What they are really looking for is that breakthrough opportunity to find a better way to eliminate or reduce the costs involved. Earlier in the meeting I talked about DELL computers in Austin, Texas. They found they could sell computers directly to consumers at very low prices by advertising in computer magazines and taking orders by phone or mail. No retail outlets to fund and manage, no multiple warehouses thus reducing overheads."

"DELL has expanded again by being one of the first people on the Internet where people can build and then buy their computers direct."

"Again Marketing is identifying the new consumers shopping trend of using the Internet and finding how it can most efficiently distribute their products through it."

"What is the real idea of this channel of distribution or place?" Asked Sarah, "I really want to simplify this area."

Peter answered, "Simply put, the best channel or the best place for the product should achieve the broadest exposure to the target audience. This means if we take a product like gum, we want to find it in every place people stop to purchase any type of grocery product, or convenience product, or impulse product. This is why we have seen the expansion in the gas stations of various products in the grocery item area. They are providing the opportunity to provide additional exposure of the product, in this case gum, to the target audience."

"Why? Because people are pumping their own gas and, walking into the outlet to pay, they have the option to buy those kinds of things, like candy, magazines or chocolate bars at the register."

"It will also depend on the kind of product you manufacture. If it is a broad product that is needed for convenience, such as paper clips or newspapers then broad scale exposure and broad distribution is required."

"If it is something that has either expensive or limited appeal, then selected distribution with few sales people and a few distributors will satisfy. For example surgical equipment. This is only sold to surgeons in hospitals or clinics, a very narrow distribution target. Again Marketing can make those analyses or reviews and develop the strongest possible set of plans to capitalize on the information generated."

"OK", said Sarah quickly. " Now we finally got it, Marketing can set up the most financially sound and efficient way to get the products and services of CONE Inc. out to our customers. Great!"

"Distribution can also be used to offset competitive moves." commented Peter.

"Lets go to DELL once more. Their competitors thought they had found the way around DELL since DELL did not have any retail outlets."

"Yes." nodded Adam, "that was one of their key success criteria."

"But that was only until DELL did their marketing work and decided to attack their competitors," said Peter.

"There is a group of businesses called Value Added Resellers," continued Peter, " They are large firms like Anderson Consulting or EDS who recommend solutions to company opportunities. They recommend DELL and sometimes they load the equipment and supply it to their customers. DELL picks up the after market technical support."

"So distribution and Marketing are really key. Now I see Marketing's role. Any last thoughts Adam?" Sarah asked quizzically.

Adam thought over his comments then stated, "Historically we just moved the products where Sales found customers. Since we had unique products that worked. Now I feel we missed many opportunities by not taking advantage of this marketing area of distribution".

Adam opened his green book. "If I was to sum up this area, I would say the distribution we have now equals the current sales volume times the revenue minus the costs equals our opportunity profits. But Marketing can identify incremental distribution, create plus volumes, and generate profitable business opportunities."

"Additionally, Marketing can strengthen the sales opportunity by focusing on real customers. By analyzing the characteristics of the product and the customer we can segment the market. This will provide us the option of identifying the strongest segments or groups of customers to focus the Sales Force effort. This is a real ROI approach to business."

"Excellent, I could not have done a better job at identifying the real business opportunity of distribution!" exclaimed Peter. It was really exciting to see how Adam had captured the core ideas of today's discussions.

Sarah also shared the infectious enthusiasm that had been created in the discussion today.

On a flip chart Sarah had written the equations. As they all studied the notes the pattern was clear.

"Let's remember that Marketing terms like any business discipline can have several meanings." Commented Peter. "When we hear people talk about the 4P's they will talk about Place. We have been talking about distribution. They are one and the same."

Adam opened his note book and wrote our CONE Inc. current model looks like this:

Current distribution + sales volume x revenue - costs = profit

---

The new CONE Marketing approach would look like this:

Current distribution + incremental distribution

+ sales volume + incremental sales volume x revenue - costs

= profit + incremental profits

$$CD + ID + SV + ISV \times R - C = P + IP\,^{©}$$

"Yes, Marketing would help us take advantage of the place elements," Adam stated to the group.

With that summary they all gathered their notes and left for the day. Each had their own thoughts about this Marketing discipline and the benefits it could bring to CONE Inc.

11

Adam and Sarah met over the weekend for a casual drink and discussion. They had set up a backyard BBQ at Adam's place and their respective children and spouses were having fun splashing about in the large inground pool.

"Thanks for taking the time to do a little business on the weekend Sarah. You know I don't normally like to do this," commented Adam.

"Yes, but we are making great progress understanding this Marketing area, and it is worth the half an hour of our time right now to be set up for the next meeting with Peter," stated Sarah.

She looked out the glass doors and saw her husband playing with their two kids in the pool and turning to Adam said,

"All right. In the next meeting with Peter we said we were going to talk about pricing and you asked me to think about that since it is one of the areas that Finance focuses on."

"The thing we have to understand Adam, is pricing is a great many different things. We have our physical products and the raw materials and the costs to manufacture. But there are also (when we look at the external items) discounts, trade or functional areas, allowances, and there are price level guarantees, a whole variety of techniques. It is really a much more complex area than simply setting some pricing."

Adam thought, 'Yes, and part of the problem is every sales person working with a customer, sets his or her price plus, the distributors have their individual pricing parameters.' Out loud he said, "It is much more complicated than just setting the price as you said."

After a few more items of discussion Adam and Sarah joined their families to enjoy rest of the BBQ fun.

12

At the next meeting, this time held in Peters office at the university, Adam started the conversation.

"You know Peter, we have a pretty good handle on this pricing area. Sarah is an expert in terms of Finance and we have a good handle what our costs are, so I don't know what Marketing can add to pricing?"

Peter started with the following comments. "I would like to ask you a couple of questions. Does each sales person set the price they need to get the contract?"

"Does each retailer set their price or do you provide some parameters? And does a customer have the option to buy at more than one place?"

Sarah started to answer, "Well we know what our costs are and we give those guidelines to Sales. To your first question, Sales can set a customer by customer price."

Adam also commented, "You know, customers can buy some of our products retail through the wholesale channel. They can also buy them direct, and sometimes those prices are different. Now nothing illegal, but I am just beginning to realize there are some differences."

"Lets set up a definition of pricing so we can all talk from the same perspective," Sarah said in a matter of fact way.

Peter wrote on the flip chart, 'Pricing is the exchange of monetary revenue for goods and services between a company and an end user or purchaser.' ©(6)

"Fine", commented Sarah, "That is a core definition to help us all build a common concept."

"I have another couple of questions," remarked Peter. "What is the competitive level of pricing? What are the competitive allowances and discounts? And who tracks all that?"

The silence hung in the air as both Sarah and Adam were deep in thought, pondering the questions raised. It was then they realized they didn't have an answer to this very important question. They felt an excellent job had been done of pricing internally and they did get some feedback on occasional contracts, but there was no one in charge of gathering information and analyzing it.

Adam broke the silence by saying, "You know, we don't really track competitive information and analyze it to any great extent, except on a contract by contract basis."

"Let me ask another question," said Peter. "Do you have a pricing strategy for each product or product line? Do you have pricing strategies for your products or strategies for your services at CONE Inc.?"

"Well no, we price each on what it cost, and what kind of profit and what markup we want." answered Sarah.

Adam felt a light coming on, "You are right, we are always pricing it based on discounting and sales," he said out loud. "However, if we set a pricing strategy it might be more effective and we might generate more revenue."

"Exactly," Peter interjected. "A pricing objective seeks to get as much profit out of the market as possible. What we have to realize is, there are various pricing areas and various ways of looking at it."

"However, a pricing objective and strategy will help us, regardless of where we are geographically, whether it be around the corner or around the globe."

"We also have to think of the whole area of product life-cycle again, where the product is in the cycle and how much can we charge for it. What are we trying to do in terms of moving the product out the door. A number of items must be analyzed and decisions taken."

"Let me ask another question," Peter continued. "How many different pricing strategies do you think there are in a basic product pricing strategy?"

Adam answered, "An educated guess? There are 4 or 5 basic pricing strategies."

Sarah added, "Yes, 5 maybe 6."

Peter pierced the air with the answer, "There are over 16 different pricing strategies that can be used! And this is one of those times when different strategies overlap." [5]

"Really" mumbled Adam "I don't really get that."

Peter answered, "For example, let's take airline tickets. There are seasonal discounts, there are group discounts, there are pre-booking or timing discounts, there are corporate discounts, and there are distance discounts. So there are five different strategies for one pricing item, an airline ticket, and there are plenty of other examples."

Adam began to think, 'This whole pricing area is much more complicated than we have imagined, and it really needs to be tied together with some of the other business issues. In fact, it really is an important part of Marketing to understand all this.'

Peter said enthusiastically, "You could also be looking at pricing by market segment or pricing by channel. All of those options could add additional revenue or volume."

"Pricing by segment looks at the way a product is used and by whom. Marketing then analyzes whether the segment can be priced differently. For example you could price a product for the consumer home office segment that buys one or two items at one level. For the same product, a different price for the industrial office segment that buys a hundred units at one time. Maybe the home office product is a box of paper at $29.95 per box, while the industrial office that buys 1,000 boxes in one order of the same paper, is at $22.95 per box."

"Wow," said Sarah, "I'm really having my eyes opened as to how Marketing can help and influence the pricing strategy."

"I also see how Finance can work with the Marketing, as can other people, in order to build the information we all need to make a good analysis and eventually stronger profits. The key characteristics of a segment can mean more volume and more revenue. "

Peter followed with, "Let me summarize. If you really think about this whole pricing area, there are a variety of policies and pricing objectives that can be used. They can be focused on a profit orientation, a volume orientation, or a following orientation."

"It will depend on the market conditions, competitive requirements, flexibility of the customer end, the product life cycle and a number of other elements like discounts and actual costs. Pricing itself can change significantly and requires a number of analysis, right Sarah!"

Sarah said, "Yes, there are things like break-even analysis, demand analysis, cost analysis, and several other things that sometimes we do and sometimes we just don't have the time to do."

Sarah continued, "Each one of those formulas can be used to impact the overall pricing. Sometimes, though, I think we don't really look at what we are trying to do strategically beyond the formulas. The formulas cover the inside issues. Marketing can help by looking at the outside influences such as competitors, customer expectations and other items"

"And that is really the key," said Peter. "We need to look beyond these techniques and pull it all together in terms of what is best for the product and what we can actually attain from the customer."

"It would seem such a simple process," stated Adam, "but obviously it's much more complex when we start talking and looking at it from a Marketing perspective."

"Very good," laughed Peter. "You are starting to talk like a Marketing person."

"Well, I am beginning to think as a Marketing person," replied Adam joining in with a laugh.

They left the meeting after setting up the next one to talk about the fun area of Promotion. Peter had provided some information of the sixteen pricing strategies.

Adam was lost in thought for some time. He began to think of pricing for the various CONE Inc. products.

He began to run through the sixteen pricing strategies Peter had outlined in the material he had provided at the end of their meeting. There was skim pricing where you price a product high when it is introduced to help set the top of the market. This is the strategy most electronic companies follow with products like VCR, camcorders, cell phones, and other.

Then he looked at the list, there was bundling, that was where a company links several products or items together. Why, maybe they could bundle the service contract and the products together, yes that is another pricing strategy option to explore. Why, just look at the computer industry! When you buy a computer it is bundled with programs, and warranty and a service option.

After several minutes he realized that the key pricing elements needed to have a group or person responsible if they were going to maximize the pricing strategies for CONE Inc. products and services.

Out of the desk came Adams green Marketing binder. It was time to put some of these key thoughts down on paper.

He stopped for a moment and looked out the window. It was still sunny and the day was as bright as the future.

Pricing is the exchange of monetary revenue for goods and services between a company and an end user. [7]

Current Pricing x Volume = revenue

There are at least 16 different strategies

Customers + Marketing Pricing x Volume = Revenue + Additional Revenue

$$CU + MP \times V = R + AR \,^{©}$$

This Marketing was more complex than he had originally thought.

But when he looked back through his notes there were more pluses and exciting ways to generate more volume, revenue and profits. Yes, he could see the next level of Marketing for CONE Inc. It really needed some integration into the company processes and systems.

13

As Sarah sat in her office early the next day, she thought to herself, 'This is probably the area I know least about. I know all about number stuff, but when we get into advertising and promotions and public relations, it's all kind of a blackhole - how do I know what I'm getting for my money or my time. I'm not really comfortable with all this. It's not as fact based as I'm used to.'

'The way we spend money on those trade shows for example. And what do we really get out of it?'

Then she began to look around. Advertising and promotion was really everywhere!

The accounting industry trade magazine was on the corner of her desk. It usually had some excellent articles in it every month. The more she thought the more the fog lifted.

She worked on the month end trial balance for a while. As she stopped, she went and got a coffee. That was when she noted the name of the coffee supplier on the coffeepot.

This made her laugh. For all those cups of coffee she had she did not think she had really noticed the name on the coffeepot. 'But I must have', she thought.

Then she remembered going into the grocery story on the way home last night. The end aisle display had a giant poster of a lady and her dog. The Ralston Purina poster had captured her eye and made her stop as she was on her way to the checkout counter. She had stopped and bought a bag of the new Dog Chow with Lamb & Rice, for her dog Rex. So a poster had sold some product.

Maybe there really was an ROI to advertising and promotion. 'Fine,' she thought, 'let's get this CONE Inc. month end wrapped and then off to the movies with my husband.

14

As they walked toward the meeting room at CONE Inc., Adam said, "This is the fun area Sarah. This is where we get to create things, develop brochures, create trade show exhibits, and it can really be a lot of fun."

"Right," said Sarah, "It may be a lot of fun but I don't really understand the value of it."

Adam had gathered up a number of product brochures, advertisements, trade show materials and sales tools, and he had put them all on the walls in the room, so when Peter arrived he could see the great stuff they were doing!

Peter walked in and looked around the room. He was amazed at the variety of materials and the different ways they had approached things. "What an excellent set of material, Adam. You and your company are to be congratulated!"

Adam started with, "Peter can you give us the thinking behind this Communications area, more from a big picture point of view, before we actually get down into talking about some of the finer details?"

"Certainly," Peter replied, "let's start off with what is Communications? Communication is the method by which persuasive messages, either externally or internally, about the product or service, are delivered to people. We can break this area down into four different major elements."

"We can talk about the Message, the Message Vehicles, Promotions and Public Relations." ©(8)

"This is interesting," said Sarah. "I never even thought about breaking it down before."

"Actually, breaking it down," said Peter, " is critical to understanding what is to be developed, when to develop them, and how to use them."

He continued, "For example: The Message is what's said or shown to customers and potential customers. It is what they have to look at and helps them understand what we are trying to do with our product or service. It suggests to them the benefits of product or service"

"The Message Vehicles are the medium or the way we choose to deliver the commercial message. These are things such as magazines, newspapers, posters, and sell sheets."

"Promotions are short term incentives or stimulation programs. They are set up to quickly generate sales."

"I like that," interrupted Adam. "Generating sales is important. We should do more promotions Sarah!"

"Wait, wait, wait," interjected Peter. "Let's understand that we have to do a mix of Marketing efforts, not just pick one and run with it."

"All promotions will only drive short term business but won't build long term business. For example, if your product is always on discount people begin to believe that is the everyday price. Look at the cereal people with those inpack premiums or on-pack offers. Does always doing promotions really generate long term volumes? No!"

"Interesting point," added Adam, "Okay, Peter please carry on with your comments."

"Promotions are short term incentives and they include things like direct mail, telemarketing, seasonal discounts, volume discounts, coupons, sales contests, trade shows and a variety of techniques. But remember they are short term in nature. It fact that is what is key to understanding where they fit in the overall mix of communications elements."

"Public Relations is non-paid for communication, or third party endorsements, Press releases, articles in business magazines or consumer magazines, articles in newspapers, can all be examples of that."

Peter paused to let it sink in. As he had stated each one of these examples, he had written them on a flip chart so he would have a focal point for their discussions.

"The next point I want to write down," he continued, "is how a balance of the four elements is needed to create an overall plan which effectively supports the product or service."

He put a big oval around that and said ,"This is really important. If you are doing or focused on one area only, you are providing information only one way, and, remember, people or customers gather information from a number of sources such as magazines or TV, and areas such as discussion with friends, print media or lifestyle situations."

"Yes" said Adam "but that's why we have the sales group, they go one-on-one with our customers, or they get the retail person organized and they are very effective."

"I don't doubt that they are very effective," said Peter, "however , we have to remember that not everyone has the opportunity to get one-on-one with a sales person."

"Another key factor to add to the overall equation is part of the decision someone has made or is going to make about buying a product or service was already made before they get to a sales person."

"A 1993 study done by the DRG group showed that when corporate buyers made a decision to buy a major item, they picked one or two items they were already aware of to evaluate. [9] Equally important, a survey done in 1992 showed that many buyers bought items they already knew and had brand equity in their minds." [10]

"Other studies have been done on consumer products and still others on services. They all support the same principles. People will learn then go buy."

"We are going to talk about brand equity later on, but just understand the balance or mix is what is critical."

Peter continued, "I would like us to think of the ad that was originally put out, I believe by McGraw-Hill in the early fifties. It showed a man sitting in a chair with a scowl on his face and he said something along the lines of 'I don't know who you are, I don't know your company, I don't know what your company products are, I don't know what your company stands for, I don't know your companies service record, now what is it you want to sell me?"

"People won't buy a product if they have never heard of it. So what we have to do is figure out a way of helping people understand what it is we have to offer."

"All right," said Adam, "but how do we know when to advertise, and how do we know when to promote or use Public Relations?"

Peter answered, "Well it all depends on the Marketing Plan and what the objectives are. The plan will help you decide the balance. It will also tell you the kind of advertising, promotion, or public relations to use."

"For example: we could be trying to develop a product that is very early in the life cycle. We are looking for primary demand or trial purchases. So therefore we need pioneer or information advertising and then promotional programs."

Sarah joined in, "Why would you need less promotion? I don't understand that."

Peter turned to her and answered, "If I give you $10. off something that you know nothing about, like say, a glue gun, there is no real value in the promotion for you." "So $10. off something you don't need or know anything about is of no value to you. There is no value perception from which the customer can evaluate the discount. There is no real incentive to take any action."

"However, if you have some awareness of the product and have some perceived value, then the promotion can trigger movement or action."

"So," Peter continued, " you really have to look at what the particular target audience is, in terms of the consumer response models. For example if we use the awareness, interest, evaluation, decision and confirmation (AIEDC) model as the elements of what a consumer goes through, for each one of those levels we need to do a different kind of advertising."

Sarah stated. " But everybody knows about CONE Inc. and our great products!"

"That's true," added Adam. "You know we are one of the pioneers in this industry and people know a lot about us."

"That could be true" said Peter "But remember, there are new people entering the market all the time. There are new marketplace opportunities where you could expand, and they may not know about CONE Inc. What you really need to do is research."

"This is all part of what Marketing people are supposed to do. They gather information about your market and potential markets to evaluate it. Remember when we talked about the product life cycle in terms of where the product is on the curve. Now you can see how it impacts advertising and promotion as well as pricing and distribution."

"Very interesting. This was good learning. Now tell me more about Public Relations," said Adam.

"Great," answered Peter, "I think Public Relations is one of the least understood elements. If you think about PR, it is actually third party endorsement."

Sarah asked, "Can you expand a little on third party endorsement."

"Certainly," continues Peter. "Third party endorsement means it is not an advertisement, so I, as the reader, don't consciously screen it out, as you might do with an ad. You have often seen headings in newspapers and start to read them and then realize what you are really reading was an editorial which supported a specific product or service."

"If you think about Trade magazines, anywhere from 40% to 60% of the material in them is really Public Relations releases, edited to fit the magazines needs. The focus on a company can create added awareness and interest amongst the core target audience for your products."

"All right," said Adam. "I am beginning to understand that we need to do Public Relations. But because we have trade shows I feel we don't really need to advertise all the time."

"A balance, everything is a balance in Marketing" stated Peter. "What you really need is a PR plan. You don't need to necessarily pour lots of money into the plan. But the structured plan will let you see all the elements."

"But if we advertise, do a trade show, do direct mail and telemarketing all in the same month and then do nothing in the month after, or the next month after that, we may have wasted our effort."

"The idea is to keep the awareness level or the opportunity for awareness open, so whenever a customer turns to looking for the item, they have a high level of awareness. Then they can move to the next level in the purchase decision model, the level of interest."

"Think about the last time you went into a Walmart or Home Depot or any grocery store and you had to buy an item you don't buy very often?"

"Other than the store brand what brand did you consider or perhaps buy? Think about it for a second." said Peter quickly.

Sarah thought about going into Walmart and she had to buy candies for her kids. She had naturally gone to a Mars product rather than the generic Cluff candies. She felt she had a handle on the quality of a Mars candy product.

Adam thought about going into the grocery store to buy a cake mix for his son's birthday. He had automatically gone to Betty Crocker without even looking at any of the other brands of cake mix on the store shelf.

 Betty Crocker was the first brand he had remembered. So he jumped in saying, "Yeah, when I think about buying a cake mix for my son's birthday, I would buy Betty Crocker- it is the brand I know."

"Now I don't buy cakes very often but, obviously, advertising has influenced me, because that was the one I bought and didn't think twice about it."

"Exactly my point," commented Peter. "Now, while those are consumer product options, the same goes for the area of industrial products or services. We go to the companies we know because they already have some equity, some value in them which makes our decisions easier. That makes it harder for competitive sales people to get in there and gain store or shelf space. Again, if I don't know what your product or service is, I don't know what you stand for. There is a lot more evaluation required than if I know those things."

"Okay," agreed Adam. "Suppose I have this great ad, how do I know where to put it?"

"There are many different options and it comes back to what is the strategy. Where does your target audience see things? What is the most efficient medium to buy?"

"Ah," reflected Sarah, "efficient, I like that. Cost efficiency even in advertising is important."

"Absolutely," agreed Peter. "Advertising sometimes is called the black hole and therefore it must work twice as hard to show it's efficiency."

"Yes," Adam added quickly, "How can we measure advertising efficiency?"

Peter thought for a moment. "This is an area where you have to be careful. You can spend a lot of money to generate just some nice-to-know information. Given the size of CONE Inc. at the moment, doing research to know the total effectiveness of your advertising could be difficult. We need to measure advertising awareness before the ads come out and after the ads come out."

"But tracking it directly to a sale can be costly and time consuming, and may not be necessary till you are much bigger and have bigger ad budgets".

"However, direct mail, promotions and trade shows - a number of things can be evaluated right through to 'what did we close and what sales did we generate'."

"For example with direct mail you could have a coupon or 800 telephone number. With a promotion you could track the number of entries. With trade shows you could gain qualified leads that translate to sales."

Peter felt it was time to introduce another concept. He looked around at the advertising and material covering the walls. "If you look at these materials," he started, "they are reasonably professional, so you had them done at an outside source?"

Adam answered, "Yes it is one of the things we are proud of. We have an ad agency that we use to do our creative and sometimes they do the media buying for us."

"Let's look at these two items here," Peter continued. "This is obviously an ad in a trade magazine."

"Yes, that was in the leading trade magazine. We got the outside back cover," stated Sarah.

"Great," said Peter, "and this was the brochure used at the trade show?"

Again Adam answered, "Yes, and it won an award at that Trade Show!"

"Excellent! Do you notice they don't quite look the same? There are different type faces, and therefore different ways you talk about the product."

"Yes," replied Adam defensively, "and what is your point?"

Peter was ready with his answer, "Well you want to have the same look and feel in all your communications. You notice there are two different logo's for CONE Inc. You want one logo is used everywhere! And this is what Marketing has to do as part of integrating elements."

"They have to make sure that there is a consistent formatted message, with the same look and feel in any medium with any media."

"Now," Peter added quickly, "it doesn't mean each ad has to be identical, or set up cookie cutter style. It means every time I look at something from CONE Inc. I know what it stands for, and that it is a CONE Inc. product. Also the product has its own individual feel. Your product lines all have to have the same look. Here look at this product line you have here," he said pointing to the wall again.

"Oh yeah, our Sierra line," explained Adam.

"You'll notice how it doesn't really look like a line? It looks like several individual products which happen to carry the Sierra logo at the bottom!"

"Yes, you're right, and that's because each brochure was completed as each product was created. Putting them up on the wall, really shows the differences" Adam explained.

Sarah laughed and then related the story of how she had gone into the grocery store and seen the poster which reminded her of an ad she had recently seen in a consumer magazine for new Purina Dog Chow with Lamb & Rice.

"Exactly," reinforced Peter, "That was leveraging the same creative or advertising in two places. It is a very cost effective use of advertising."

Peter looked at them both and saw that they had taken in a lot of information for the day and thought it best to summarize now. So he quietly continued, "This whole area of advertising and promotion seems simple. Just think what you need and develop it. But it is not that simple!"

"What you really want to make sure is: you have consistency of message; you have the right target audience focused on; the product positioning is being clearly communicated - in the advertising and promotion. It is also important that all the materials have the same look and feel for the product, or the family of products."

"When we look at this whole area of advertising, it should impact the sales. Promotions should generate short-term sales, but it's only one of the elements of the Marketing Mix' and it's the balance of all the elements which will generate incremental volume, revenue, and profits."

"One last area to think about for promotion," stated Peter, "Is demonstrating a return on the investment of advertising."

"Yes!" jumped in Sarah. "Yes ROI in advertising!"

"To do that you need to set up data base Marketing which captures target prospect information for use in focusing your media efforts," added Peter. "You should be adding an 800 number to your advertising and setting up a data base for all those warranty cards and really using it."

"For example Seagrams went to the publishers of several magazines and asked to put ads in by subscriber. They set up postal walks and had certain ads for postal walks ABC and certain ads for other postal walks DEF all in the same edition of the magazine. This targeting of the message will get you a stronger ROI for you advertising dollar."

Adam sipped his now cooling tea and looked at both Sarah and Peter and said, "I now understand that this is a more complex area than I did a couple of weeks ago when we started all of this. But I still need help in understanding how we can manage it easily within the organization. Can you give it some thought Peter and at our next meeting help us understand how we can manage this process?"

Peter answered, "I would be glad to."

"I have been involved with several companies in terms of creating the systems to manage this, for now, we will call it the Marketing Product Management System. I have helped develop the processes and procedures, with outside people, to make it very effective. Let me put some thoughts together and let's meet tomorrow or the next day."

Sarah turned to them both and said, "Let's try to meet tomorrow while the momentum is going. I get the feeling we can see the end of the tunnel here and I, for one, would like to get there."

"Always the driver," chuckled Adam. "Great, all right let's look at our schedules. We could probably clear late afternoon, if it is good for everyone else? Why don't we do it back here and make this kind of our business Marketing room for now, then we can leave the material up and any other charts or graphs we create."

"Okay," said Sarah enthusiastically!

"Sounds good to me," added Peter cheerfully!

As they walked away from the meeting, each of them had their own thoughts. Peter was having a good feeling he was helping to create some real value in a good company. Plus, as agreed with Adam, he would be able to use it as a test case for his academic work. So they were each getting some significant benefit out of this.

Also, it was helping him organize how he was going to approach the new course he was creating for business entrepreneurs.

This had been a long session. But it made Adam realize the area of communications was key to any company. It had to be understood and not underestimated.

Adam had many notes to add to the green Marketing binder that day. The definitions and letter formulas helped him to see the applications clearly. They also helped to focus the information. And lastly they helped to make all this new data usable in building the value of the business.

In the communications area there are the Message, the Message Vehicles, Promotions and Public Relations.

You need to have a consistency of message, that you have the right target audience focused on, and that the product positioning is being clearly communicated to for effective communications.

Message + Vehicle Message + Promotion + PR =

Effective communication plans

M+VM+P+PR=ECP©

Effective communications + current sales efforts = +volume

Now it was becoming obvious that this area of Marketing

needed to be managed to be effective. He was looking

forward to Peter's thoughts on how to do this.

15

The following meeting, held in a room at CONE Inc., had been set up by Peter to talk about how to manage this process of Marketing within a company. He had prepared for this meeting by making Adam and Sarah understand that without the use of specific Marketing tools, key business building decisions could not be made.

He had prepared some charts for the meeting making it easier in directing the meeting and overall discussion.

Adam had had some time to think and was starting to have some concerns this was going to create a great deal of overhead and human resource issues without actually creating any more business value.

He had e-mailed the concern to Peter and asked him to address it at the next meeting, to help decide the steps to be taken on this key Marketing project.

Adam stirred his tea and looked up at Peter and said, "Please help me understand what we should be doing next, what the logical steps are, and what the real value is here?"

Peter answered, "What we need to understand is, there is a value which I will call 'Marketing Equity'©. Let's define Marketing Equity so that we understand what it is and how to value it for your products."

Sarah liked the concept and voiced her thoughts. "Yes, I really need to put some parameters around the value is of this Marketing and the managing of it."

Peter said, "Let's start with the concept we need a central group to manage the whole Marketing effort. Usually, they are called Product Managers or Brand Managers. Product Management responsibility falls into several key areas. Overall the Product Manager becomes the intelligence centre for the products or services.

They do this in the following ways: [11]

1. Understanding the customer needs through a number of strategic steps.

2. Analyzing the product or service on an ongoing basis to confirm progress against specific objectives and strategies.

3. Identify alternative courses of action required to maximize programs and the product itself.

4. Provide clear concise communication both internally and externally to help those resources understand how they can improve the product.

5. Increase the product's value to customers through the successful use of all elements of the Marketing mix."

Sarah said, "Okay I'm beginning to understand what these Product Managers do, but what do they actually create beyond some of the physical things in the Marketing mix we have talked about, such as pricing or advertising or promotion?"

" I need to understand their value as well as their cost." Sarah continued.

Peter answered her, "I would like to give you another definition before we get into the definition of a Product Manager. We need to know what Marketing Equity is in terms of a definition so we can build a complete perspective."

"We will define Marketing Equity as the total value Product Management can generate for a product or service, by managing customer needs and expectations using Marketing Tools, Techniques and Practices." ©[12]

"The total value of a product is not just the price paid. If we take the example of Sunkist, in 1993 they licensed the Sunkist name in the United States for 10.3 million dollars. [13] They had the Sunkist name on fruit juice, candy, and as an ingredient in a variety of items. People believed there was added value in using the Sunkist name. That was the Marketing Equity [TM] value manufacturers saw in licensing just the name Sunkist."

"When large companies are sold, there is goodwill attached to them, multiples of book rates that don't equal just the physical values of bricks, mortar or resources. The same is true for a product. That is what the Marketing Equity ^{TM} is for a product or service."

"The Product Manager is the key person for driving that."

"We can take it another step. Product Managers' values are the assets and liabilities linked to their efforts and the plans they generate. The plans add or subtract from the value provided by a product or service to its users, potential users or customers or potential customers."

"Measuring value comes in a number of ways. It can be the level of brand awareness that allows Sales to make sales easier. It can be the repeat purchase business that comes in by phone or fax. Orders which are generated without a lot of effort add sales volume, extra revenue, incremental profits and overall equity."

"Now we need to define what a Product Manager is in Marketing."

"Okay," said Adam, "Let's start with the definition of what a Product Manager is, if I can understand maybe it will work for me."

"It is really built off the definition of Marketing," Peter continued, "because Marketing is what the Product Managers do."

"One definition I've found successful is the following." stated Peter. He stood up and wrote it on the flip chart.

'The Product Manager is the Business Champion who drives the product forward through analysis, decision making, and coordinating programs, using Marketing mix elements and tools to satisfy present and potential customer needs, while generating volumes, revenues, and profits within corporate guidelines.' ©[14]Copyright S.Rayfield 1999 All rights reserved

"I'm beginning to get a picture of this person," commented Sarah, "I think I need to identify some items, and then you tell me if this is what a Product Manager does."

Peter smiled, the light bulbs were beginning to come on and they were starting to drive the process.

Exactly what he had hoped would happen. He took a sip of his warm coke and said, "Okay Sarah, write down some things on the old flip chart."

Sarah wrote 'The Product Manager is the person in the organization assigned the responsibilities for overseeing the various marketing functions concerning a product or service.'

"Yes! Very good," said Peter excitedly.

Adam rose to the occasion also and moved to the flip chart, tea cup in one hand, pen in the other. "I think, it's also, well let me write this down." 'The Manager of the Marketing mix elements for the product or group of products.'

"Very good," said Peter. "I think also, let's write this down," and he rose up and started to write below what Adam had just written on the chart. 'It's the person who determines what direction a product should be going and uses the required Marketing or business tools to reach those goals.'

"Right," said Adam. "Now I am beginning to get a real picture of this person. There must be some elements of successful product management that we should look at."

"That's right," answered Peter. "Product Management has been around for a long time. It really started in 1931 at the consumer products company, Proctor and Gamble, where they wanted to have products that were competitive within themselves. They felt if they could generate their own competition that would generate more volume, revenue and profits." [15]

"Equally important though, they wanted to have someone who could take the Marketing effort and coordinate it, provide budget commitment, work with Sales, and work with the internal departments of the company to focus efforts to create Marketing Equity."

"A study done by the Boston Consulting Group showed how leading brands between 1925 and 1985, of 22 different categories they looked at, 19 had the same brand leader after 60 years. [16] In two categories the leader dropped. In one to number 2 position. And in one category the leader had dropped to 5, but in all cases all products were still viable contenders in their various markets."

"So generating Marketing Equity becomes very important, and the Product Manager is the person charged with that responsibility."

Having stated that, Peter sat down. Sarah smiled and started, "You know, I think I'm beginning to get it completely. If Marketing is attempted by many different people in the company, without the central focus that has the control and authority over it, we are not maximizing our Marketing Equity. In fact we could be making poor decisions and hurting our Marketing Equity."

Peter replied, "Looking at David Ackers book on Managing Brand Equity' [17] we see that one of the ways Brand Equity is hurt is when 'there is no person in the firm who is really charged with protecting the Brand Equity.' Also, there's no long term strategy for the brand or product. We are not creating a mental image which will be stimulated in the future. We are also not evaluating or analyzing the impact of the elements of the current Marketing program."

Sarah asked a key question. "How can we really identify this Marketing Equity element?"

"There are a number of ways it can be done," Peter answered. "One of the examples would be to research a branded versus unbranded concept. While this has been done by a number of people, it has shown they can generate a lot more money. For example: American Motors tested a car called the Renault Premier, by showing an unnamed model of it to potential customers in research and asking what they would pay for it."

"The same was then asked with the car identified by various names. With the Renault Premier name on it, it generated a premium price of almost 32% more or $3,000." (18)

"When Chrysler bought American Motors, the car became the Chrysler Eagle Premier and was sold for a price close to the level suggested by that study. This is a specific example of Marketing Equity generating incremental revenue and profits."

"Okay," said Adam, "I'm starting to see there is value in Marketing Equity, but I am still not convinced the Product Manager has to be there."

"Product Management is essential." replied Peter "I cannot emphasize this enough. Let me repeat it is absolutely essential. When people have dual roles they move towards the one they are the most comfortable with. Would you agree with that?"

"Yes," answered Sarah, "Look at the Sales people who like selling while getting them to do financial reports or their expenses is really difficult." Everyone laughed.

It had been a rather serious meeting up to that point but now the true-life real examples were bringing some interest and some reality to the table.

"That's right," Peter followed, "and what we need is someone who can be that champion as we said in the definition, to drive it forward."

"I think you are right," Adam added, "We really need to have that function focused on a particular individual. But I also need to understand what they can do. I would like to absorb what we have talked about so far, I don't know about you Sarah, but this is a lot of information for me. Now we have some very serious decisions to make."

"Yes, you are right," Sarah replied, "but I have a good feeling now, I understand what Marketing is, why it is important for the company. Now I have an idea about the value it can bring to the company. I just need to understand more about processes and techniques."

"Why don't we have a meeting in a couple of days?" asked Peter. "I also think we are getting to the point where you people have to decide if you are going to introduce Marketing into your company and how you're going to do that. I have some thoughts we can discuss next time."

With that the meeting broke up and they left the CONE meeting room. Sarah walked Peter to his car.

"I can't thank you enough Peter for the work you are doing. It is really helping us to understand what we should be doing and I think it will move the company to the next level."

Peter looked at her smiled and said, "Thank you for saying so, because that is really what Marketing can do. Depending on where a company is, it can move it to the next level of business."

Peter continued, "Thank you for letting me work with you on this. It has given me some good insights into how I should shape my 'Entrepreneurs Course' for next semester at the university. I have worked with large corporations all my career. Working with you has helped me understand there are not really big differences in needs. Just a different set of zeros after the sales dollars in the annual report."

Sarah walked back to the building and had a much better feeling about where this major project was going to go. Equally she could see how their business could benefit.

Back at his office, the CONE Inc. green Marketing binder in hand, Adam made some meeting notes. He now was very glad he had started the notes when he did. They would form the basis for the next step of implementing the business case for the marketing process.

In the quiet of his office he started to write.

Marketing Equity = Total Value of a Product or Service

(ME=TVP)©

Marketing Equity must be built and protected

Marketing Product Managers = Product Champions who build and protect Marketing Equity.©

Well, that was very interesting, he thought. Now it was starting to take form and show what they had to do!

16

Sarah walked into the meeting room, "Sorry I'm late, I had to finish off my last meeting and it ran over a little."

"No problem," Adam said as he thought back to the conversation he had been having with Peter regarding the next steps that were going to be taken on this project. Earlier in the day he had met Sarah in her office and they had talked casually about the fact this was a very important project for the future of the company. Therefore they had to start putting some form around it.

"At the last meeting we asked the question of all three of us," started Adam, "what does a Product Manager do, and how do they operate? Looking at the definition, we know they analyze, make decisions, and coordinate programs."

"Well, from my perspective," said Sarah, "I think it has to be a group of individuals who have some responsibility for a particular group of products. They have to be given Marketing dollars in order to do research or development or use external resources."

"Very good," commented Peter. "You have a good handle on where this is going. Equally important, however, they have to do an analysis of ongoing business. Product Management isn't always future looking. Analysis has to be done in order to provide learning, understanding and tracking of the existing marketplace and efforts."

"So what we are saying," said Adam, "is we need a separate business unit, which has specific Marketing responsibilities and procedures established."

"If I was to summarize some of the key areas," said Peter, "I would look at the overall planning area. They need to do product reviews and develop Marketing plans."

"They have to have specific templates and formats they use to plan and communicate the objectives. They need specific processes documented so they know where they are going."

Sarah looked at the group and said, "I also think they need to have the support of Senior Management. Seems to me that to be effective, they are going to have a lot of responsibility without the authority. The support of Senior Management is going to be imperative if this is going to work properly."

"That's right," added Peter, "this is very important."

Adam turned and said, "It's clear we have to set this up appropriately and, Peter, you have been a tremendous help in getting us to where we are today. We understand clearly what Marketing is, why it is important to the company, and the most important thing that Marketing generates is Marketing Equity in products and services, if managed appropriately."

"That equity can come in terms of added value, premium pricing, broader distribution, greater volume, increased revenues and ultimately greater profits."

The rest of the meeting consisted of discussions on the processes and procedures of how this could be set in place at CONE Inc. so it would add value and create the least disruption. Adam felt that he was going to need some help from Peter in order to establish the correct criteria for people who should be involved.

Equally important Adam said, "Now that we understand this Marketing area, we need to get the executive committee to understand and buy into this whole process. Once they have understood and accepted the process, then we can set up the required training for a formal Marketing structure and formal Marketing processes and techniques."

Sarah smiled and echoed the words Adam had said earlier to her, "This is the business key to moving the company forward, to solid growth and to become more competitive in the long term."

Adam also said, "Peter, I would like to summarize some additional thoughts Sarah and I have had. Over the past few years, management has looked at corporate planning. We have identified our culture and created a mission statement. We think that's a good base for moving the company to its current position. Would you agree?"

Peter answered, "Yes, that is an excellent start."

Adam continued, "Now we have to create some expansion while managing the products and services. This means getting a champion, called the Product Manager, to create that Marketing Equity.

"This means grouping the brands, doing strategic planning, working out the portfolio matrix tools and various tools and techniques for a key procedure. The strategic programs, techniques and policies that you use will be very important in moving you to the next level of volume, revenue and ultimately profitability," stated Adam with confidence.

Peter spoke up, " I would like to introduce one last concept to tie this together. It is Integrated Marketing. [TM]"

"We need to be careful people do not just think of this new direction as something someone else must do. A solid definition is '**Integrated Marketing is the ability to move marketing from a department function to a core business competency for all company functions focused by Product Management.**" © (19)

"This goes beyond just Marketing by the Product Manger. It includes everyone in the company understanding that Marketing is a part of all that is done, but focused by Product Managers." Concluded Peter.

It was agreed Peter would start working as a consultant to establish (for the executive committee) the true definition of Marketing for CONE Inc. and to ensure it's properly communicated and understood internally.

Adam thought, 'This all started with Sarah and I trying to figure out how to move this company forward, knowing we were doing a number of things right. But now they are going to do things in a Marketing way through Integrated Marketing!"

Adam moved to the flip chart and began writing, " If we look around we can say:

1. CONE INC has moved from one product to many products. With Marketing we can segment the products and the market. We need to analyze the product mix on a regular basis to decide which product to keep and which to cut.

2. We have a solid management team in place that works well together. Marketing can give them fact-based information on customers needs and direction, while helping senior management to make fact based decisions.

3. Sales are working hard and we have seen they really try. Marketing can provide key sales support tools and stronger targeted new products.

4. Our products are a mix of different share levels in their various markets and are really all great quality. Marketing can review those markets and the competition to see how we can grow our volume, revenue and profits.

5. The people in the company seem motivated. Internally, Marketing can build on that. An internal PR program would be a great start.

6. Our client list is growing. Marketing can make sure they are the right clients. Marketing can also identify the opportunity clients, plus ways to expand our products.

7. And our distribution is solid. Marketing can confirm what are the right channels."

Then he added, "Now we have the concepts, and the direction, we can really grow the revenues, volumes and profits. This is really key to the next stage of future growth for CONE Inc., doing things in a Marketing way."

He had shown the CONE green Marketing binder to Sarah earlier in the day. Now he opened it and made one last note.

Integrated Marketing is: Current Products + Marketing Core Competency + Product Champions = Increased Revenues and Profits. ©

CP + MCC + PC = IR+ IP ©

"Now, that is what business is all about" he said with his Presidents hat on, "Profits!!"

Closing the CONE Inc. green Marketing binder, he looked around the room. "Thank you all for your insights, comments and hard work on this important business project. It has been an interesting learning experience. I feel confident it will help us grow to the next level of business."

Then he stated enthusiastically, **"This is why we need Integrated Marketing now!"**

Afterward or
Next Steps/ Indicated Actions

Having completed the journey of Integrated Marketing ^{TM} discovery at CONE Inc. you have a greater understanding of why you need Integrated Marketing at your company. You also understand that you may be doing Marketing at your company but not as effectively as possible. To manage and increase the product and service equity, let's start the business building process now!

So what should you do now to take advantage of this to grow your company volumes, revenues and profits?

You must begin by analyzing your level of Marketing effectiveness currently in your company.

This will then identify those key areas that need to be improved or modified to generate the strongest Marketing effort for your company.

Send for the ESIL Marketing Effectiveness survey. It's free, so that is effective and cost efficient. It will take about 30 to 45 minutes of your time, or anyone else in your company who completes or fills it out, and we strongly recommend several of your key people complete it, to give a solid overall perspective of your company's current Marketing efforts.

The Marketing Effectiveness survey is self-scoring. It will also provide you with three areas of action. Naturally we would like to help you do this. But even if you do not use our services you will be able to increase your Marketing effectiveness just doing the survey.

To start your journey call ESIL, 1-888-ESIL-374

(1-888-374 5374) or use the coupon in this book or fax ESIL at 1-416-225-0027. There is no obligation to us at ESIL, only to your-self and your company.

Start to improve the Marketing Equity ^{TM} of your products and services with Integrated Marketing ^{TM} now!

R. Stephen Rayfield

North York Ontario Canada

Notes for the curious
John Jakes set up his final information with the heading 'notes to the curious.' in his book *California Gold*. I found it intriguing and thus have borrowed the idea from him.

1. Pg. 15 Stephen Rayfield, *The Marketing Effectiveness* survey 1998, is an ESIL technique to discover the level of Marketing usage at a company.

2. Pg. 25 C. Davis Fogg, *Team-based Strategic Planning*, AMACOM 1994

3. Pg. 39 For more information on this topic see Y.H.Furuhashi and E.J.McCarthy, *Social Issues of Marketing in American Economy, Columbus*, Ohio: Grid, 1971, pp4-6

4. Pg. 59 Stephen Rayfield, *Definition of Marketing*, ESIL, June 1996. This is a basic definition.

5. Pg. 69 There are many definitions for product this is a simple one to focus the discussion. For more information see *Basic Marketing*, McCarthy, Shapiro, Perrault latest edition Irwin Publishing or any basic Marketing book

6. Pg. 89 Note in several AMA courses. *Fundamentals of Marketing* AMA Jim Carlton and Stephen Rayfield 1997

7. Pg. 100 Stephen Rayfield ESIL *Marketing User Manual* 1996. Pricing is key but rarely defined

8. Pg. 104 Stephen Rayfield ESIL *Marketing User Manual* 1996. A review of the Marketing mix elements.

9. Pg. 108 International Data Group, *Buying OT in the 90's: The Channels*, Boston 1992 pg. 83.

10. Pg. 108 International Data Group, *Buying OT in the 90's: The Channels*, Boston 1992 pg. 87.

11. Pg. 125 Stephen Rayfield, *Marketing User Manual*, ESIL, May 1995

12. Pg.126 Stephen Rayfield, *Marketing User Manual*, ESIL, May 1995

13. Pg. 126 David A. Acker, *Managing Brand Equity* The Free Press 1991 pg. 8

14. Pg.128 Stephen Rayfield, *Marketing User Manual*, ESIL, May 1995. Definition of a Product Manager.

15. Pg. 130 David A. Acker, *Managing Brand Equity* The Free Press 1991 pg. 5

16. Pg. 130 David A. Acker, *Managing Brand Equity* The Free Press 1991 pg. 8

17. Pg. 131 David A. Acker, *Managing Brand Equity* The Free Press 1991 pg. 9

18. Pg. 132 B. G. Yovovich, *Adweek's Marketing Week*, August 8, 1988, pp. 18-24

19. Pg.142 Stephen Rayfield, ESIL, May 1998. Definition of Integrated Marketing.

INDEX

Survey Order Form

Please send _____copy(ies) of "ESIL Marketing Effectiveness Survey:" now! The survey is free, and does not require me to buy or contract ESIL for anything. The results of our survey maybe shared with ESIL but only in the strictest confidence.

My Company Name: _____

My Name: _____

My Address:

_____

City: _____

Prov. /State : _____Postal Code/ ZIP_____

Country: _____

My Telephone: _____

My Fax : _____
My business is (just a few words to describe your business)

_____

_____

_____

Please send to
- ESIL Fax: 1-416-225-0027
- Call our toll free North America phone: 1-888-ESIL-374
- Postal : ESIL Publishing, Stephen Rayfield, 213 Franklin Avenue, North York, ON M2N 1C8 Canada

About You!

Do You have any comments on this unique business book?

Send us your success stories of how it helped you! Just send by fax or email the changes that this brought about in your company, its systems, or approaches to marketing. Let us know how it worked and the valued it generated.

Or if you have any thoughts on how to improve the book for the next edition. We would be glad to hear them.

Just send your thoughts to Stephen Rayfield, ESIL, 213 Franklin Avenue, North York, ON M2N 1C8 Canada or phone 1-888-ESIL-347, (1-888-374-5347) or fax 1-416-225-0027 or email at srayfield@ibm.net. For all the ideas we use, we will be glad to give you credit in the edition they appear in, plus three free copies!

Do you know anyone who could use this book? Please let us know that too, and we will be glad to send them copy with a covering note from you.

Survey Order Form

Please send _____copy(ies) of "ESIL Marketing Effectiveness Survey:" now! The survey is free, and does not require me to buy or contract ESIL for anything. The results of our survey maybe shared with ESIL but only in the strictest confidence.

My Company Name: _____

My Name: _____

My Address:

_____

City: _____

Prov. /State : _____Postal Code/ ZIP_____

Country: _____

My Telephone: _____

My Fax : _____
My business is (just a few words to describe your business)

_____

_____

_____

Please send to
- ESIL Fax: 1-416-225-0027
- Call our toll free North America phone: 1-888-ESIL-374
- Postal : ESIL Publishing, Stephen Rayfield, 213 Franklin Avenue, North York, ON M2N 1C8 Canada

About ESIL

ESIL is a North American firm whose goals are to develop and increase marketing skill's sets of key organizational people through creating specific company learning programs and individual coaching sessions for the people. This seeks to leverage the product or service marketing equity, of the people, of the products, and for the shareholders.

ESIL is the Interim Marketing Development company dedicated to improving your ability to maximize your Marketing Equity through Integrated Marketing.

We generate Exceptional Strategies Innovatively Learning based on our marketing business experience, everyday work within the business environment, and our ability to use current best practices and the most successful techniques of world class companies.

---

*We have chosen the PineCone to represent
the ESIL philosophy.*

Each PineCone has many seeds and each represents to ESIL the
seeds of learning waiting to be nurtured.
PineCones are always on green trees no matter what the climate
or weather showing a positive approach to any issue.
The pinecone symbol represents the fresh spirit of personal
learning and individual growth.